From Clueless to Success

Back stories from my journey in Communications

Adedoyin Jaiyesimi

Contents

3

Gratitude Wall

In writing this book, I experienced an overflow of gratitude towards everyone who has played a key role in my professional journey. This Gratitude Wall serves as a reminder of the fact that I arrived at the door of success through the support of many, many people.

To My Abba, the One who owns my life, thank You for calling me higher. Thank You for leading me on the most beautiful journey ever.

To Francesca, my Mainest Mentor and Sister! Thank you for being there through it all. Thank you for being one of my biggest cheerleaders.

To Mrs Tara Fela-Durotoye, thank you for listening to me when I was clueless and paving the way for me to begin my journey in communications.

To Chude Jideonwo and Adebola Williams, thank you for taking a chance and giving me the opportunity to learn, grow deep roots and do great work.

To Isime and Stanley, thank you for that night in Port-Harcourt that you did not allow me to throw in the towel. Thank you for being there.

To Tolu Orekoya, thank you for taking your time to make sure I didn't become a mediocre writer. It really made a difference.

To Sola, Damilola, Emilia, Bukonla, Daphne…thank you for all the great memories!

To Rev Victor Adeyemi, you believed in me when I was unsure of myself. Thank you for always popping your head over my cubicle to check on me!

To Pastor Jumoke Adeyemi, thank you for ingraining excellence into my DNA. I see the fruit of all our staff training.

To Pastor Goke Nathaniel, thank you for having faith in my ability to occupy that special role at Victor Adeyemi Ministries.

To Pastor Taiwo Odukoya, thank you for the opportunity to serve. Thank you for all your prayers and your confidence in me.

To Pastor Tolu Ijogun, I am grateful for the opportunity you gave me to use my gifts to serve TFOLC and Pastor Taiwo.

To Dotun, Dunsin, Chiebuka, thank you for staying with Content Craft until the very end. I think we did great work together; don't you?

To Mrs Osayi Alile, thank you for reading and responding to my DM that evening. Thank you for giving me the opportunity to serve.

To Mosun Layode, thank you for the push to send in that application. Thank you for believing in me and trusting me with large projects.

To Mrs Aishah Ahmad, Mrs Adeola Azeez, Mrs Ronke Onadeko, Mrs Hansatu Adegbite, thank you for the encouragement and faith in my ability to deliver.

To Olori Boye-Ajayi, thank you for always speaking into my spirit and ensuring that I become everything the Father has destined for me to become.

To Aunty Alero, Pastor Emmanuel Dania, Pastor Tonye Cole, Aunty Imo, Dean Udy Ntia...thank you for showing me what unconditional love looks like.

To Oduola, I love our Batman and Robin work dynamic. I treasure the gift of your friendship and your unflinching support.

To OTD of life! Thank you for giving me the chance to swim in bigger waters. Thank you for your support, come rain or shine. I love you Mama E!

To Sharon, thank you for showing me how to charge for my services. Thank you for being a source of support in this transition phase.

To Sarah, Tobi, Ife, Tutu…thank you for the great conversations during APF events. APF continues to have a soft spot in my heart.

To The Comms Avenue Community Members, thank you for trusting me as I navigate this ship. I don't take your kindness for granted.

To Deedee, the one who has been there through it all, the one who listened to me and stood up for me. Thank you for being the best brother ever.

To my parents, Mr Lateef Oladele and Mrs Modupe Jaiyesimi, I'm grateful for all the sacrifices you had to make.

To all the clients I had the privilege to execute briefs for, I'm grateful for the opportunity that you opened up to me!

To everyone who encouraged me, opened a door for me, believed in me, referred me to a client, and recommended me in rooms where I was not present, I am super grateful. Thank you!

Introduction

2020 makes it officially eight years that I've worked in the communications field.

Eight years? Time does fly.

Wasn't it yesterday that I found myself back in Nigeria with a law degree, an unfinished Masters' degree and no clue whatsoever concerning what I wanted to do with my life?

I had little motivation and no clear direction.

All I could think about was - "Where do I start from? How do I begin to put together the broken pieces of the well-planned life that I had created for myself?"

My family had suffered a huge financial setback. That's why I had to return to Nigeria in the middle of the Masters' program at Cranfield University. All I had was my writing skills – a divine gift that I had not appreciated before this point in my life.

Little did I know that this precious gift was going to change my trajectory and allow me to thrive as a communications professional.

This gift paved the way for me to work as an in-house communications manager. It also allowed me to do freelance gigs, run a communications agency and eventually, create a community for communications professionals across the world.

I've had a good number of highs and quite a number of significant lows. I've been broke and confused. I've also been fulfilled and determined to make it work. This book gives you a peek into the things that have happened behind the scenes within those eight years.

I have written this book with gratitude in my heart to God for making all things beautiful. Every story in this book is significant. It is a reminder of the capacity God has given to me. It is an acknowledgement of the fact that I couldn't have been a successful communications professional without the help and support of friends, mentors and angels. I was completely clueless when I started but somehow, the journey continues to unfold beautifully.

I hope you enjoy the stories and learn from my journey too!

SECTION ONE

IN THE

BEGINNING

How it all started

"I don't know what I want to do with my life!"

These are not the words you utter while sitting in front of a successful entrepreneur who has invited you for a mentoring chat.

I will confess. I uttered those words and I meant it with my heart.

As an undergraduate at the University of Leeds, I had mapped out my post-uni career plans. They were very grand plans, none of which included relocating back to Nigeria.

Yet, there I was, in this beautiful office, wondering how to answer the question Mrs T asked about my goals.

I had to be honest. I had no goals or plans. My life had been disrupted and I didn't know how to get it back on track.

Then she went on to ask me what I could do. I didn't have to think too much to answer that one.

"What I really know how to do is to write. I can do it from sleep."

For as long as I can remember, I have always loved reading and writing. Writing was a form of therapy for me. Literature was also one of my favourite subjects in secondary school. I've always been in love with words and the power they have in shaping narratives and perspectives.

That being said, never in a million years did I think I could build a viable career from writing. I mean, I wanted to live the rich and glossy life. I didn't know any writer in Nigeria at the time that was living that kind of life. That path was, therefore, not an option for me.

And that's why when Mrs T started to speak to some people over the phone about an 'aburo' that loves to write and wants to intern with them, I was a bit confused.

"Internship? But I didn't say that's the kind of job I want."

Of course, I didn't speak these words out. They remained nicely locked up in my thoughts.

When she asked me, some minutes later, if I wanted to do full-time or part-time, I was still dazed when I gave my reply. "Full-time."

"What will a career as a writer look like? What's the hope of making it big? Wait, what exactly is going on here?"

My thoughts were all over the place but somehow, I remained still.

"They need you to send in an article you have written and they'll take it from there."

I didn't even have an article or story because I hadn't done any personal writing in years! I thanked her and left her office, still a bit confused but willing to take a chance with this writing thing.

Plus, what did I have to lose? I was an intern at an HR Consulting firm that paid me 20k every month. I knew after the first month there that it wasn't something I wanted to do for the rest of my life but it was a good job to have after weeks of depression when I abruptly returned from the UK.

I got back home, brought out my laptop, opened Microsoft Word and began to type the words "The Journey to Fulfilment". You won't believe I still have that article!

I completed it in less than an hour and I sent it off to the Chief Editor of YNaija and another media platform.

I closed my eyes and tried to picture what this new route will look like. Am I making a mistake? Should I just call Mrs T and tell her that this is not what I want to do? But what was it that I really wanted to do?

There were many questions flying through my head as I tried to figure out what my options were. With every question, a layer of fear gripped my heart. You know that fear that usually comes when you want to venture into the unknown. It was heavy and suffocating.

I looked through my email hours later and there it was. A response from YNaija. Someone was going to contact me to schedule an interview with their editor. This response only made me more anxious. I was about to step into the unknown and I wasn't even sure what the final destination would look like.

There was no way I could answer the questions in my head, however, without trying. This was the moment. To take the leap or not.

I plunged in! After all, I really didn't have anything to lose. I had already hit rock bottom.

Adedoyin's Nuggets

It's ok to be clueless when you begin your professional journey. In fact, at different stages in this journey, you may still feel clueless because life comes with its curves and bumps. You must, however, be willing to take a risk, be open to learning and be curious enough to move into new territories.

Many of us are too paralysed by perfection or the fear of what people will say. I have learnt that people will always talk. That's not something you can control. Shut out the noise as you try to figure things out and resist the urge to explain your journey to everyone. They will eventually get it when your blooming season arrives.

Enjoy the clueless phase. Worry less and give yourself room to explore the fullness of your potential!

Getting my first by-line

"Did I ask you to sit down?"

You know how they say you don't sit down during an interview until you are asked to? Well, I think there is a rule like that. For whatever reason, I entered into Partner A's office at Red Media on the day of my second interview and I presumptuously sat down.

Don't blame me. I had waited in the reception for a while and when I eventually entered his office, I think I had been standing for two minutes before I decided to just sit down. Ok, maybe not two minutes but it was long and it was awkward.

Of course, that attempt to sit down was futile. The look I got when he said those words, "Did I ask you to sit down" should have prompted me about how that interview would go because it went downhill from there. In my opinion.

He invited me to sit down and we proceeded to have what I consider to be the weirdest interview of my professional journey. I didn't understand how the questions he was asking me related to the internship I was hoping to get. For example, he asked me why I was putting on all black (this was before black became my favourite colour). I said the very first thing that came to my mind. "I am wearing black in memory of the victims of the Dana Crash; a number of them were acquaintances." This wasn't far-fetched as the Dana Crash had happened two days before the interview.

"So, what you are trying to say is that you wear your emotions on your sleeve?"

"It's like I have entered one chance with this man!" I thought to myself.

And so the interview continued. I mentally told myself to forget this internship. Aside from the very strange questions, he looked quite irritated on the few occasions he took his eyes away from his laptop and looked at me. It was with great gladness that I jumped up when he said, "That will be all."

As I planned my escape from the disaster that had just unfolded, he added, "By the way, I hope you know that we do not pay our interns." Yes. I had heard it countless times since I started the process. I nodded and told him goodbye.

I got home and I burst into laughter when my brother asked how it went. He looked at me and said, "It was that good?"

"No, actually it was a disaster." At this point my brother was confused and after I gave him the summary of the interview, he said something like, "There will be others."

A few hours later, the editor I had been engaging with from the beginning of the process called me to get my feedback. I was honest with her. She listened silently as I recounted how badly I believed I had performed.

"Well, he loved you. You just have a final chat with Partner B but we're more or less going to bring you on board as an intern."

This time, it was my turn to be eerily silent. How could that be possible? When I eventually found my voice, I asked for the details of the final chat and I thanked her.

The final chat with Partner B was a glaring contrast to the interview I had with Partner A. Partner B mentioned that it was an intentional strategy to weed out incompetent applicants. I was still puzzled but I nodded nonetheless.

I started as an intern the next day. My colleagues were quite warm and they welcomed me nicely. What I didn't find welcoming was the amount of effort I had to put in before my first article was published on YNaija.com. I had to devour pages of magazines such as Vanity Fair, GQ and several others and I also had to visit a number of popular new sites daily to read their content.

I have to thank the editor I worked with during the initial days of this internship, Tolu Orekoya. She could have stopped at telling me my work wasn't up to standard and asking me to re-do it. She took it a step further by telling me why. She would take the time to edit what I did and ask me to compare with what I had sent in and then send her an email with my observations. The difference was obviously clear. I also had the privilege of asking her why and sharing my thoughts if I didn't agree with a particular edit.

We did this for about three weeks. I'll admit, it was frustrating. Every time I thought to myself, "This is the one. Today is the day I am getting published," Tolu would flag something else or say, "We're not quite there yet but you're making great progress."

It was comforting but it wasn't enough.

I will never forget the day she approved my news article to be published. I think I cried when I read the words, "By Doyin Jaiyesimi" – my first by-line. I still remember the exact content. It was a story about the video of a song that Chuddy K released that day, "Gaga Crazy." I can't say exactly what inspired me about the song but I poured my heart into that 300-word story.

"That's more like it! You're ready. Well done."

I listened to Tolu's feedback with joy and gratitude.

That was the moment I knew I had found my water. I felt validated. I had finally discovered a place where I could thrive. I was a fish that had been struggling on land for years, with the ever familiar feeling of being lost. A meeting, a conversation, and a doubtful yes, all led to that moment where I finally realised there was a lot more I could do with my writing gift.

And I was ready to dive in and swim fully in this water.

Adedoyin's Nuggets

You should never lose hope or jump to negative conclusions before an official decision has been made. Even after the official decision comes, I have seen over the years that as long as God is in it with me, that official decision will either be reversed or something better will open up.

This means faith is an essential part of the journey of success as a professional. Faith allows you to take one more step, to try one more time, to send one more email. Faith in myself made me stay the course. I kept at it until I finally had my by-line. The process allowed me to become an exceptional writer and editor. I'm glad Tolu didn't let me get away with being a half-baked writer. She ensured that I was a fully-baked and diverse writer. I didn't realise it then but Tolu mentored me informally. Having access to mentors who are deliberate about helping you to hone your skills is critical in your journey.

Don't despise the baking process. It's there to refine you into the best version of yourself.

Hawking magazines on the streets of Lagos

"I didn't send you abroad to be hawking magazines on the streets of Lagos!"

One would never have thought that my name and 'hawking' would be used in the same sentence but there I was, listening to my mother complain about what I felt was my innovative attempt at making sure the magazines I worked hard to produce did not die a painful death in the store.

How did I get here?

After three gruelling and intense months working as an intern at YNaija, I was offered a full-time position as a Staff Writer. It felt good to hear the

HR manager tell me that the partners wanted me on board full-time. It meant I was doing something right. The internship period wasn't without its fair share of drama and stress. August was particularly daunting (I'll share the backstory next) but I made it. I survived.

Few weeks into the Staff Writer role, Partner B told me that he wanted me to shadow the Copy Editor of the company's magazine with the long term goal of running it eventually because he believed in me. I thought I was hearing double. I had always been fascinated with magazines. While my friends were collecting beauty items and jewellery as a teenager, I filled every empty cupboard with magazines and books. However, to be asked to run a magazine at a time when I was just finding my rhythm as a writer was not something I had anticipated.

If you ever interact with Partner B, one thing that will leap out strongly is his passion. He painted this very nice picture that really appealed to my inner pursuit of purpose. I said yes, silently praying it would not end up being a mistake, with me killing his precious magazine. Yes, that magazine was precious to him.

And so I started to do the shadowing thing. If I haven't said it before, the early days of my professional journey involved being thrown into the deep end. Frequently. I found myself in another deep end when the Copy Editor had to leave abruptly and I had to more or less take charge.

I struggle to find the words to describe my state of mind in this new role. A part of me loved it. Every challenge came with an equal dose of confusion and adrenaline that made me bold enough to believe I could find solutions to the unexpected problems. There were many, many sleepless nights. Emails upon emails reminding contributors to send in their articles because the deadline to go to press was drawing dangerously close. Missing deadlines at some point was a given! Despite all the careful planning, something always went wrong or didn't go as planned.

And then there were the cover shoots. Handling celebrities and their drama were some of the least enjoyable moments for me. I still recall one that told me to pet her dog because it had malaria. I'm still confused by that action eight years later. There were definitely tears in all of this. Losing valuable content. Shoots going off tangent. Oh, and I received quite a bit of unsavoury insults too.

The experience was a mixed bag of everything but somehow, I enjoyed it. Seeing the final product, the printed edition of the magazine that I had sacrificed sleep for, holding it in my hand, reading the stories, seeing the press mentions online and how people responded to the content - it kind of made everything worth it. That joy never lasted too long, however, because we were on to the next edition with little or no time to pause.

There was one thing I didn't particularly like though. After all the hard work and stress, somehow we were not selling as many copies of the magazine as I had expected. I remember going into that store, seeing the boxes lying there on the floor and saying to myself, "No. All this work cannot end up like this. This cannot be it." But I was clueless about the whole Nigerian magazine distribution process. There were agents and street vendors. There were the campus reps and there were stockists. Distribution always gave me a headache.

"What can we do better to make this magazine sell?" That was always the niggling question in my mind. We had significantly improved the content without straying too far from Partner B's vision but it still wasn't flying off the shelves. I sat in meetings with agents and some popular magazine editors just to understand what we could do better. Partner B wanted to crack it. So did I.

In my clueless state, I resolved to take some boxes of magazines home and become a street seller. Where did I get such an idea from? I can't really answer. At the time, I just wanted to try something different. So I took copies of the magazine and went off to cajole vendors at the Maryland bus stop, Anthony under bridge, Allen roundabout, Muri Okunola, and some inner roads in Victoria Island. Sometimes, I would spend hours talking with these vendors as I tried to ginger them. As long as they carried it and displayed the magazine in the top three position, I would have stayed there all day. Ok, maybe not all day.

In this experiment of mine, I walked a great distance under the hot sun, sweating and looking like I was homeless. It was in this state that one of my mother's friends saw me and immediately called her. "I just saw your daughter now hawking magazines in Victoria Island."

As I scored major victories that day and for the rest of that particular edition of the magazine, a storm brewed at home. My mother never hid the fact that she disliked my job and my complete lack of direction in life. How could I have studied Law in a university abroad, finished with a distinction in law school and was at some point doing a Master's degree in Finance and Management at one of the prestigious universities in the UK, only to come and say that I am a writer, who now 'hawks' magazines? It didn't sit well with her. My hours were round the clock and the pay was not what my peers were earning in banks and oil companies. She couldn't understand why I couldn't go for what she considered to be a more befitting job. I didn't know too but I knew that I had to take the risk to find my purpose. I was far from the desired end goal but I just knew that I was on the right path. One day, it would make sense. My mother unfortunately did not believe in dreams.

It was tough balancing the home front and a job that was all-consuming. Not having the support of your family, especially in the period when you are trying to find your way, can be a burden. I look back and thank God for His grace because He was my anchor in that season. The times I thought I would just give up, faith kept me going. There were a number of milestones like being promoted to the role of Assistant Editor and then overseeing a vertical that was launched for teenagers. Yet, it was hard to shake off that feeling of not knowing what I was doing or where my life was heading.

I look at the magazines I worked on with fond memories today. Yes, I still have them and I always will because they remind me that the woman holding them was crazy enough to traverse the streets of Lagos, just to push up sales. They remind me that I have the capacity to achieve the impossible and they also remind me of Partner B who took a huge risk to commit his precious magazine into the hands of a 22-year-old who had no idea what she was doing. Somehow, I was able to have three published magazines under my belt, the very last one being one of my favourite covers because it was a labour of love and it also marked the end of my foray into the world of conceptualizing and publishing magazines.

Adedoyin's Nuggets

Success will take you on paths that will not always be the smoothest. You can choose to be defeated by the mountains and the portholes or you can choose to pull up your boots and trudge through. I chose to march through uncharted territory with three things in my bag – my writing gift, grit and God. By the end of the journey, that bag was overflowing – with wisdom, refined expertise, tougher skin and the satisfaction of having yet another mountain demolished.

If you want to achieve great things in your professional journey, you must be bold enough to dare to walk uncharted paths. When you get to the end of that path, you will look back and realise that you have paved the way for others to follow. That's when you will become a professional who pioneers the new.

That moment when I was ready to end it all

"Excuse me ma, please are you on drugs?"

Usually, when people ask you if you are on drugs in this part of the world, it is never a good thing. This may be the first time that statement was embedded in what was intended to be a compliment. And a voice of concern.

I still remember the exact moment when the security personnel made that statement. We were in Golden Tulip Hotel, Port-Harcourt, in front of the elevator on the second floor. I actually don't blame him for asking me that question. He had seen me run from floor to floor, room to room, back and forth for hours. I guess when he saw me come out of the elevator on the second floor for the third time in 10 minutes, he couldn't take it anymore. He was genuinely concerned about my well-being. He asked the popular question that we usually ask in conversations where we have nothing else to say – have you eaten?

Why was I running around a hotel in Port-Harcourt with energy like a woman on drugs?

I was there on an official assignment. My first trip to that state. My first encounter with the behind the scenes hustle and bustle of organizing a big award show. "Messy" is what I can use to describe it. If I thought my internship was deep water, this part of it was sinking sand – not the posh kind. Thick. Brown. Mud!

The drama started back in Lagos. Everything appeared to be chaotic in the office for some reason. I didn't get it because it was my first time being involved. I observed, listened and tried to make sense of it all. There was another problem. My parents did not want me to go on this trip. My mother totally objected. "What are you going to do in Port-Harcourt? What award show?" Yes, I was old enough not to need my parents' permission but I was extra careful when it came to anything that involved flying and going to somewhere new. The least I could do was to let them know where I was going. I had to call my father to step in and he had many questions. I answered all and he tuned out when he heard 'government'. Partner A had to find time in his busy schedule to have a long conversation with my father; to convince him that his daughter was in safe hands.

I don't know what Partner A said to my father but he said yes and my mother aligned. That's how I found myself on the plane bound for Port-Harcourt. I had done my planning based on the task list that had been posted prominently on our staff notice board. You couldn't miss it. I reviewed my plans as we drove to the hotel from the airport, wondering which of them I would work on first. I mentally prepared myself for the unexpected but I didn't prepare enough apparently. The moment we arrived at the hotel, all my well laid out plans unravelled and the quicksand experience began.

Somehow, I found myself running around the hotel trying to assign guests into rooms, making sure they were fine, dealing with contingencies I wasn't prepared for, moving from one mental blow to the next. Maybe I was on drugs because I remember being in a constant state of light-headedness and wooziness. I didn't even remember the original reason why I was there – to curate content for the website.

When I thought I found a moment to quickly close my eyes, another problem reared its ugly head. Guests had gone on a full-day tour but somewhere along the line, we dropped the ball on food. You know how important item number seven is! And you know what they say about a hungry man. They weren't ready to listen to anything, neither were they concerned that I needed them to be gathered for the next event at the scheduled time. My head swirled. Empty hall. Angry people. Livid boss. "Adedoyin, think!"

Somehow, my colleagues and I were able to douse that fire and got hundreds of guests transported to the venue; although slightly later than planned. The award ceremony itself was a blur to me. I remember wanting to hide in my room. I remember asking God not to let me collapse as my heart palpitated heavily behind my chest. The one thing I looked forward to ended up going south as well.

We had the privilege of getting designer dresses to wear for the event. I had gone to the showroom of a popular Nigerian designer and she fitted me into a dress that I fell in love with. You know when you put on a dress and you have already seen in your mind's eye how you will slay and make people swoon when you step into the hall. The dress was that great. It was the only thing that kept me excited about this journey.

When I picked myself up to prepare to follow the last batch of people heading to the venue, I looked forward to looking good in that dress. Hair done. Makeup done. It was show time! As I zipped up the dress, I noticed it was a little snugger than I remembered. Of course, I couldn't have added weight in just five days. So I continued to zip up until it happened. I heard that pop sound and felt the dress going loose.

"This zip did not just spoil!!" I thought to myself.

Some of my colleagues tried all sorts to get it fixed. Nothing worked. Time was running out and I had to show up at the venue. I had no other choice but to put on the dress I had worn the day before. It was the only other piece of clothing that was appropriate for the occasion. Of course, this further dampened my already frail motivation. I wore the dress, kept my head up and went to the venue. Like I mentioned before, I don't remember what happened there. I'm not even sure I took any pictures. My mind was somewhere else, longing for my bed in Lagos.

I heaved a sigh of relief when the last batch of guests got on the plane heading back to Lagos. We spent some extra days in Port-Harcourt for a review meeting and a training. That review meeting is my most vivid memory of this particular part of my journey.

Heading to the meeting in a different hotel in Port-Harcourt, I was apprehensive. I didn't achieve 40% of the things I had set out to do. I dropped the ball completely as I sunk deeper and deeper into the quicksand. The feedback was tough. It felt as if someone pierced my heart with a dagger, right in front of me. The tears were protected by the thick walls of the determination not to disgrace my lineage in public. My father's words, "Be a big girl. Don't cry over such things," stung my ears. I took it all - the personal jabs, the mockery of the skill and professional ability I thought I had gained through the internship. It was hard.

I don't think I fully entered into my room when the tears gushed out like an overflowing dam. Compounded by my lack of good sleep for several days, everything around me felt dark. I concluded that I had come to the end of the road of this risky undertaking. It was time to quit. It was time to end it all. Maybe my mother was right. Maybe I was joking with my life. The self-doubt began to magnify and I sank even lower into the quicksand. This time, I didn't have the strength to come up.

I heard a knock on my door that interrupted my train of thoughts. I didn't want to open it mainly because I was a mess but I did. I'm glad I did. Two of my colleagues looked at me. Stanley said, "I know you are about to quit but I will give you reasons why you shouldn't." For over two hours, very late into the night, Stanley and Isime entered into that mud, determined to pull me out of it. I don't know why they did it because they ate their own share of the humble pie but they stayed with me until I was consumed by the light they brought. I had hope again and for the first time, I slept peacefully in Port-Harcourt. Maybe, just maybe, this phase will pass.

It did pass. Some weeks later, I became a full-time employee. A few weeks after that, I was part of the magazine team. An Editorial Assistant a few weeks later. Assistant Editor a few months later.

Magazine Team Lead to crown it all. I guess you can say I finished this chapter well.

Adedoyin's Nuggets

It is important to learn how to receive harsh criticism and negative feedback without letting it affect your self-worth. If you are like me and you pour your heart into the work you do, it's hard not to take negative feedback personally. However, do not let praise get into your head and harsh criticism into your heart.

I also think it helps to recognize the humanity of the person giving the harsh criticism. The jabs Reviewer A threw at me that evening hurt and for a while, I resented her but I had to let it go if I wanted to grow. I took on the valid parts of her criticism and I was determined to rise above my shortcomings. I needed to learn how to develop tough skin. I needed her words as a stepping stone to rise to the fullness of my capacity.

Pay attention to how you internalise and respond to criticism.

SECTION TWO

THE CLUELESS
PROFESSIONAL

The Birth and Death of Lily Rouge

"How much do you charge to write and edit articles?"

In an interview in 2019, I described myself as an accidental entrepreneur and many people wondered why. When I said yes to exploring where my writing gift could take me, I did not have any grand vision. I just wanted to do something meaningful and I wanted to survive. My family getting into financial difficulty when I was in the UK was a terrifying phase. I wanted to have my own money and I didn't want to rely on anyone for money. I had to find my way, clueless or not.

I didn't think through a lot of my decisions at this point in my life. They were mostly spur of the moment decisions. When I began to desire more than what the world of magazines offered, I started to have this feeling of unrest. I didn't see myself being an Assistant Editor or even Chief Editor for the rest of my life.

While my gift had been unveiled, the purposeful deployment of that gift remained veiled. I was itching for something else within me. There has to be more right? I didn't think I would discover that 'more' if I remained where I was. There wouldn't have been time or space for me to figure things out. So I went off to find that 'more', in a different city, Ibadan. Thanks to the National Youth Service Corps (NYSC).

Before I went off to Iseyin, I had to mentally prepare myself. I read up all I could about NYSC camps and listened to good advice from my colleagues on how to escape morning parades and the endurance walk! The three weeks' camp experience was good. Different but good. I was immersed in Orientation Broadcast Service (OBS) activities. I got out of going for the morning parade and the endurance walk and I met a guy I thought I could potentially get married to. When camp ended, I was disturbed by my designated Place of Primary Assignment (PPA). It was on the outskirts of Ibadan. I would have preferred to have been in the city centre but I had to make the most of it somehow.

Being active in the OBS, I soon had a second PPA in the Publicity Unit of the NYSC secretariat which was in the city centre. I was a key member of the Editorial Community Development Service (CDS) and I spent my time writing and editing content for the CDS and the Publicity Unit. Managing two PPAs wasn't too challenging. What was quite challenging was managing my funds. The monthly allawee (the stipend we received from NYSC) was barely N20,000 and my mother decided to support with an additional N5,000. That made my monthly income N25,000. I needed to find another source of income if I didn't want to starve in Ibadan.

I couldn't afford to rent a flat when I arrived in Ibadan. Thankfully, a friend had rented a big room and offered to accommodate me. Of course, it wasn't free. I had to pay half of the total rent. I still remember my thin mattress. It was so thin that you could feel the floor when you laid on it. Who was I to complain though? That was what I could afford. It helped that food items were quite cheap in Ibadan. My weekly menu usually included bread/garri and moin moin, tinned tomato stew and spaghetti, indomie and egg. Rice and yam were a luxury but I got to eat them thanks to the Shop4Free initiative in Global Harvest Church. I adopted walking as my primary means of transportation to save money. This earned me the name 'Johnny Walker'. I didn't mind. As long as I could save money every day, I was fine.

Despite these measures, I still needed to make more money but I didn't know how. I didn't have the skill to make anything with my hands to sell. I didn't even like selling to people. One day, as I tried to figure a way out, I received a phone call from one of the editors I had previously worked with. She wanted to know how much I charged to write and edit articles. I was immediately alert. I could make money from writing? As a freelancer? Why didn't I think of this before?

I had to tell the editor that I didn't have any rate card and I would take whatever she was offering. Yes, I know that was a bad answer but I was clueless, remember? Thankfully, she did pay me well. I don't remember the exact figure but I know it was nothing less than N60,000 for three articles. Please, from where I was standing at the time, that wasn't bad at all! I did the articles so well that she commissioned me for another batch and paid me even more than she did the first time.

Before the second time I was commissioned, I had done my research on freelance writing. I listed out the different things I could write and charge money for and then I created what I called my price list. I decided to make it very professional by registering a business name. I came up with the name Lily Rouge, created the company portfolio and I called my mother to help me register the company. She sent me some documents and told me how much the whole process would cost. Later on, we discovered that the name was not available. I decided to put the registration on hold and focus on surviving NYSC instead. I also wanted to get a clearer picture of what life as a freelancer would be like.

The feeling I had was that of someone who had found gold that needed to be refined. I believed I was on to something that would fast track my journey on the financial freedom and purpose lane. I started by marketing my services in church, still using the name Lily Rouge because I wanted people to take me seriously. I was already a member of the Publications Team in church where I contributed articles and edited our weekly newsletter and other church content. People knew I was gifted.

I started very small, charging people to write copy for fliers and radio jingles. I wrote proposals, worked on a Masters' research project, did some ghost writing and editing, mostly for a regrettable amount of money. I was paid N5,000 for the first book I edited and the author didn't even value what I did. The money definitely wasn't great but it was enough to keep a corper steady. It also didn't help that the jobs were on and off. I could go weeks with no one engaging my services and then in less than one day, I would receive a rush of requests. That's the part of the freelance life I didn't particularly enjoy. I loved to plan ahead. I couldn't plan with something I had no control over.

By the time I finished my service year, I was done with the freelance life. Yet again, I had discovered something else that I didn't want to do with my life. I still took on freelance writing briefs because half bread is better than puff puff, as they say. I was making some money but I still felt empty. I left Lagos to find the 'more'. It wasn't freelance writing. When I moved back to Lagos a year and six months later, I was still searching for that 'more'.

Adedoyin's Nuggets

My freelance phase was driven by the pursuit of money. As long as it brought in money, I would spend my precious time on any brief. Many times, it wasn't worth it. And it came at a price. I paused my pursuit of purpose and I chose to hustle instead.

There's more to who you are than your professional title. When you begin to see what you do as a calling, you will have more impactful and long lasting results. When your profession transitions from being about money and status to being about fulfilment, that's when what you do can become a platform for you to shine your light for the benefit of others.

I think it's time for a new generation of professionals to arise – professionals who put purpose above the hustle; professionals who are positioned to make Pan-African and global impact using their gift.

Pay attention to what God is calling you to do.

The suggestion that was a fluke

"Why don't we tweet our services live on social media?"

I've always been a curious person. Growing up, I listened to countless stories of how I would ask a million and one questions every day. My father was the only one who listened and responded to all my questions. No question was too stupid or silly for him to answer. I believe that has allowed me to confidently ask questions whenever I need to understand something.

It is with that same confidence that I asked the Church Secretary why the church did not have an active presence on social media. This was 2014 and more churches were beginning to adopt social media as a key part of their communications strategy. The thing about asking questions is that sometimes, you will be tasked with finding the answer or solving the problem.

That's what happened during my conversation with the Church Secretary. "Why don't you do something about it? I will speak to Pastor J and tell him we want to do a test run on Sunday." I stared at her with a blank expression on my face, wondering what I had just gotten myself into. The only thing I knew about Twitter was what I learnt from YNaija's Social Media Manager. He had to give me a crash course when he was getting queried for not submitting publicity tweets for the magazine on time.

"Just show me how it works. I'll do it, you will review and then send off to Partner B," I said to him one day. In fact, this is also how I started to learn about Public Relations (PR) from the

Communications Team but that's a story for another chapter.

Since the Church Secretary did not look like she was going to take a 'no' from me, I had to figure out how to make sure everything went smoothly on Sunday. I had my worn out Blackberry as my only work tool. I went through the Twitter handles of some of the churches that were already active on Twitter. "Ok, chronological sequence of tweets. Hashtag. Call to action. Be personable. Got it!" I had a plan. Somewhat.

It was a sceptical Adedoyin that went to church that Sunday. I said one of my favourite prayers as I stepped into the meeting hall, "Holy Spirit, help me!" When service started, I brought out my phone and typed, "Good morning. Welcome to church. We're glad you are joining us for service today" and clicked the tweet button. I continued to flow from there; through the praise and worship, the sermon, the announcements and the closing of the service. Live tweeting the sermon was tricky. I had to balance keeping up with the Pastor's pace with ensuring that I did not dent the church's digital image with epic gbagauns. I couldn't rejoice much when the service ended. Pastor J needed to give his feedback.

Honestly, I had no expectations. What consumed my mind was the fact that I did not want to mess anything up. If Pastor J decided that he didn't want me to continue tweeting, I would have been ok. Less pressure. But Pastor J did not say that. In fact, he was delighted – by the content, the engagement and the potential of what we had just started. That's how I became the Social Media Manager of Global Harvest Church, Agodi. Yet another water I jumped into cluelessly. Every Sunday, I balanced tweeting with singing in the choir and reading announcements towards the end of the service. I have always been one person who tends to have her hands in a number of things at once. I think it's a grace God has given me.

I was very diligent with the task given to me and I soon began to think of how to do more. That's another thing about having a curious mind – you want to poke the boundaries to see what more you will find; to uncover what more could be possible. I did enjoy this particular phase. There were mistakes, definitely. There were occasions when my tweets had grammatical errors and I only realised at the end of the service. There were also times Pastor J didn't like how I summarised a point from the sermon. "Today's tweets didn't really capture the heart of the message I preached," he'd say. I learnt from every mistake and feedback and did better the next week.

Even though I still hadn't figured out what I wanted to do with my life, I enjoyed giving myself completely to service in God's house. I didn't know it then but as I served diligently in three departments, I was digging deep roots which were necessary for me to handle the fullness of my calling. In fact, I was digging roots for the next assignment which I, yet again, entered into cluelessly. I moved from managing social media for the branch church as a corps member to managing the brand of the Senior Pastor of Global Harvest Church International within one year. How it happened was surreal. I'll tell you about it next.

Adedoyin's Nuggets

The status quo only persists until someone makes the bold move to do something different. That is why innovation is disruptive. It changes the dynamics of the status quo. Innovation starts with the boldness to ask the question, "Why?"

If you want to be an innovative professional, you must ask the right questions and then leverage the power of your imagination and creativity to find the answer to those questions. By asking, "Why don't we tweet our services online," I set in motion a series of events that brought innovation into the way the church communicated to a digital audience, thereby increasing its reach and influence. That, in turn, paved the way for a much bigger assignment. A lot can happen when you stay curious and ask the right questions.

Pay attention to how you can disrupt the status quo in the work that you do.

The Impostor Church Communicator

"We're looking for someone to manage Pastor Victor's brand."

When I moved back to Lagos in January 2015, after spending an extra six months in Ibadan post-NYSC, I was still clueless. For some reason, I had this grand idea of taking the ACCA exams. The details are fuzzy but I remember that I had written the GMAT exam while I was in Ibadan, with the hope of going abroad for an MBA.

When I abruptly returned to Nigeria in 2011, the Masters' program I had started was graciously deferred by the school. September 2012 came and we still couldn't afford the school fees. I remember that I had to travel to Leeds to bring back the things I had left behind. A part of me still wanted to go back abroad to study and build my life.

Maybe that's why I was quite clueless; I hadn't let go of the dream of living a successful life in the UK. Whatever it was, I found myself planning to register to take ACCA lessons in preparation to write the exam later that year. I didn't have a job at the time and the freelance jobs were still unpredictable.

Something happened that changed my direction. Again.

After service on the first Sunday of January 2015, I walked up to the Chief Operating Officer (COO) of Victor Adeyemi Ministries (VAM) and told him that I wanted to volunteer to work on our Senior Pastor's books. I gave him all the necessary details about my skills, not forgetting to mention that I managed social media for one of the branches.

I think I need to backtrack a bit. Something led to this encounter. I didn't just wake up with the grand idea to shoot my shot with the COO.

The Sunday before the Passing Out Parade (POP) for my NYSC batch, the church had a special service for all the Batch B corps members. It was a tradition. We were called out, celebrated and given a gift bag. One of the items in the gift bag was a book written by our Senior Pastor. I was curious about the title, Meaning and Miracles of the Holy Communion. A book about the Holy Communion? I wanted to know the reason why he decided to focus on the Holy Communion.

It took a while for me to finish reading the book. It was quite heavy to digest; heavier than I anticipated. The content was great but I began to ask myself, "Could this have been written in a way that would make it easier for people without theological knowledge to digest?" You can guess what happened next. My mind began to deconstruct the book and create a new flow and structure.

I went to church the next day and asked the Church Secretary, "Who puts our Senior Pastor's books together?"

"It is done in Lagos and the COO of VAM oversees the process. Why do you ask?"

Even though it wasn't the response I was expecting, I shared my observations with her. It seemed like a long shot at the time because I had now passed out from NYSC and the new plan was to remain in Ibadan indefinitely. By the end of that year, I found myself making plans to move back to Lagos. Abruptly. Cluelessly.

Since I was in the same Lagos where the COO was based, I decided to look for him after that Sunday service. At least, let him know that I exist and I am available. I didn't want to entertain the idea of being jobless for too long under my mother's roof.

"That's great. We are actually in the middle of working on three new books for Rev. Can you stop by at the office tomorrow with your CV and we will have a chat?" That was the COO's response.

I arrived at the VAM office the next day and in the middle of our conversation, the COO asked the Operations Manager to give me the manuscripts that were ready so that I could start working on them. He continued our conversation by asking a question I wasn't expecting.

"Are you looking for a full-time job? I've been trying to hire someone as a Brand Communications Manager to manage Rev's brand. Are you interested?"

"Brand Communications Manager? What exactly is that?"

I said the first thing that came to my head, "No, I'm not looking for a full-time job but I can do part-time." I cannot explain why I said that because I was jobless at this point but I had discovered over time that flexibility was important to me. I didn't want to have the crazy hours I had as an Assistant Editor. The COO said he would discuss with Rev and get back to me.

The next day, he did call. To make me an offer. "How much do you want as your salary?" My mind went blank. Charging a fee/ pricing is one thing I have struggled with consistently in my professional and entrepreneurial journey.

"How much do you want to pay?" I asked. He called a figure that I thought wasn't bad for a part-time engagement. I told him yes, with a plan to continue taking on freelance briefs to supplement that income.

Some hours later, I was invited to attend a branding session with Rev and other senior communications professionals in the church. As I sat and listened to these experts speak during the meeting, I felt out of place. Half of the things they spoke about flew over my head. Every now and then, Rev would look at me and ask me for my opinion. I cannot remember if what I said was meaningful but I gave my opinion. One significant thing that happened during the lunch break was when Rev told me that he counted it as a privilege to have me join the team at that critical time.

My heart started to palpitate! Should I tell this man that the meeting with the COO was the first time I had ever heard the words 'Brand Communications Manager'? Aside from what I had quickly gleaned from Google, I had no idea what I was meant to do, not to mention how. I got home that evening and that famous prayer, "Holy Spirit, help me!!"

I officially resumed at my new office a week later. I had to do a number of things that morning as part of the onboarding process but what I remember vividly is the Job Description (JD) review meeting I had with the COO. I saw my JD for the first time during that meeting and I began to panic. I only knew how to do four things out of the 12 items that were listed on the paper. "Should I just confess that I don't know how to do all these things and go home? It's not too late to end this now." I began to feel hot and cold at the same time but I managed to look calm.

When we finished the meeting, I was shown my office and given my work tools. The first thing I did as I sat down on my chair was to whisper, "Holy Spirit, help me." I say this prayer a lot, even today. I took some deep breaths, opened Google and typed the words 'Church Communications' on Google and for the most of that day, I read articles on best practice for church communications, downloaded many resources and subscribed to a number of useful websites.

God did help me in that role. It also helped that Rev was very open to adopting my spontaneous ideas. In fact, I did a lot of experimenting with his brand. "Why don't I create this kind of content?" "What will happen if we do early morning prayers every day?" Rev never shut down any idea. He gave me room to stretch and grow. Eventually, I had a good grasp of what worked and what didn't work. I learnt how to create a content calendar and interpret analytics. I also learnt how to use Canva to create spur of the moment designs for social media. I learnt new things such as editing audio messages for podcasts and then I began to poke the boundaries of existing templates to find out how it could be better.

One day, my curious self said to Rev, "Why is it that during our conventions, all the branches of the church post independently. I think it will be more effective if they all come together and push out content from a single account." Rev thought it was a good idea and asked me to share it with the Lead Pastor of our headquarter church in Ibadan. "Sounds fantastic, Adedoyin. Do you want to create a plan and budget for the leadership to approve and then you can execute?" I really should have been used to getting that kind of response but I began to ask myself, "Adedoyin, who sent you?"

My plan was approved, the budget was tweaked and I was given the go-ahead to implement for Harvest Fire 2015 which also coincided with the 20th-year anniversary of the church. I won't go into too much detail about the process of integrating the social media teams of over 10 branches and ensuring we worked collaboratively to achieve a common goal.

Pioneering the new is never easy. There were sleepless nights, challenges that never stopped popping up, multiple personalities to manage and so on. But, what started out as a question led to the creation of a model that is still adopted in the church today.

Working at VAM gave me wings to fly. Another thing it did for me is this – it redirected me to the path of purpose.

Adedoyin's Nuggets

It is valid to ask the question, "What will happen if this does not go well?" I think it is equally valid to ask, "What will happen if it does?"

We never really know how much we are capable of achieving until we try. When you try, you'll discover what works and what doesn't. And when it doesn't work out the way you anticipated, don't see it as a failure. See it as a new lesson learnt.

I encourage you to dare to believe in yourself. I have reached a point in my professional journey where I am confident that there's no feat that is too great for me to accomplish; no problem that is too hard for me to solve, especially when I have the Holy Spirit to help me.

You are an exceptional professional with the capacity to achieve great things. Don't let anyone tell you otherwise.

Stumbling into an
international brief

"Are you very sure you can do this work?"

By now you must be familiar with that voice of doubt that refused to leave my head as I swam through the waters of uncertainty. This time however, the voice was not in my head. It was an external voice and the question was indeed valid, "Are you very sure you can do this work?"

I wasn't sure.

When Francesca called me some days before this glorious encounter that ushered me into a new terrain, I obliged her request to go for a meeting with her boss simply because I was curious. "We have a research brief and you are the only person I know who has the capacity to deliver." Coming from her, it meant a lot. She couldn't give me too many details but I'd get to know more about the brief during the meeting.

I sat straight on the nice, cosy sofa and listened to her boss as he gave me the full details. "This is a research brief and we're looking for someone who can do detailed research on the subject matter and write excellent reports."

"Research? I can do that." The hours I spent in the library sifting through case law and reading through Lord Denning's judgment to find the paragraph that had the exact precedent for my case had equipped me with strong research skills. I've not met that many people who can get to page 12 of a Google search just to find information. Not only that, I had good writing skills. All I needed was a template and I could put together a good report. I felt good about the brief until he mentioned the client.

"By the way, this is a Bill and Melinda Gates Foundation project."

Bill and Melinda what? I experienced that woozy feeling that came whenever I felt out of my depths. "Ah, Adedoyin. Abort mission. Just tell him that you cannot do it and go home!"

Then there was this other voice. Still. Small. "But you can do this, Adedoyin. It is the same research and writing skills."

I think Francesca's boss must have perceived my self-doubt from where he was sitting because it was at this point that he started to ask if I was very sure I could do this brief. My first yes was shaky but somehow, it received strength as he persistently asked that question. I remember Francesca being in the office but I couldn't look at her. I didn't want to fall her hand.

As if I wasn't terrified enough, her boss then asked me how much I wanted to be paid. "What should I say? What should I say?" I blurted the first figure that came to my mind. He converted it to dollars and said the figure was fine. That's how I got my first international brief!

We discussed other modalities and I asked if I could get a template of the way they'd like the report to be presented. "There's no template. That's why we are engaging you. Come up with your template." It took everything in me not to collapse at this point but I kept it together.

When I got back home, I sat down on the floor and asked God to help me with the brief because I was back to that point of cluelessness. Again. Too much was at stake for me to mess things up. Most importantly, I couldn't afford to disappoint

Francesca who had glowingly recommended me to her boss, even after that meeting.

I started working on the brief a few weeks later. What I loved most about it was that I got to learn about the world of finance – financial inclusion to be precise. Every now and then, I'd have to Google the meaning of a word but I mostly got the gist of it. Since I wasn't given any template, I downloaded and reviewed at least 10 reporting templates. None of them fit exactly into what I was seeing in my mind's eye. So I decided to do a bit of mix and match to build the perfect template.

There was a tight delivery deadline and virtual meetings in between. I had to manage this with my role at VAM. This meant I had to work round the clock to make sure I didn't miss any deadline. When it was time to send the first report, my palms were sweaty and my body was itchy. "Please Abba, don't let this thing be nonsense."

Two days later, I received the feedback. "Well done. The HQ has decided to adopt your report as the benchmark for the rest of Africa." To be honest, those words did not sink in until hours later. I think I was just relieved that it wasn't bad. It was later that day that I paused and said, "Wait. This is actually big!" The template that I put together cluelessly was now the benchmark for the other African countries involved with this research. I didn't pat myself on the back for this win. I was just profusely grateful to God that He stepped in and breathed upon the work of my hands.

A brief that started out as a one-month engagement turned into a six-month engagement where I learnt how to do many new things. I worked on my first international communications plan and I also got to learn how to put together a media training.

There were some exciting one-off projects beyond this brief. Francesca never failed to recommend me when anything suitable came in. Beyond opening doors and clearing paths, what Francesca did for me was to boldly stake her reputation on my professional ability. "But you can do it." "I've told them that you are the perfect person for it. They will call you." It didn't matter that I was sweating or freaking out, Francesca believed in me wholeheartedly. And because she believed, I started to think, "Maybe I'm not such a clueless professional after all."

Adedoyin's Nuggets

How do you deal with that voice in your head that makes you believe you are inadequate? We describe it as impostor syndrome. I call it the mental mountain that every professional who wants to accomplish great things must conquer.

The moments of doubt will come, but you must always remind yourself that:

- You are capable and good enough.

- You are on a beautiful journey of growth.

- You know what you are doing.

Pay attention to how you speak about yourself and your professional ability. Your words have the power to paint a good or bad picture that can influence how you are perceived by others.

SECTION THREE

THE CLUELESS ENTREPRENEUR

The long road to purpose

"I want you to join me to build the Leading Ladies Africa vision."

A few months after I moved back to Lagos from my time-out in Ibadan, I stumbled on a post on one of my former colleague's Instagram page. It was a flier for an event that was put together by Leading Ladies Africa (LLA). It wasn't the event itself that caught my attention. It was the fact that many of my former colleagues were also planning to attend this event.

"This will be a good opportunity to see the crew again and catch-up," I thought to myself.

With that, I made up my mind to go for the event. I called Daphne and asked if I could hitch a ride with her. We met up on the day of the event and drove to the venue. On our way, she received a call from the organiser of the event asking her to handle social media because something happened to the person who was meant to do it. I listened to Daphne as she gave the summary of the conversation and I told her that I'd support her by posting on my Twitter and Instagram page. By this time, my confidence as a Communications Professional had grown and I had a good understanding of how social media worked.

When we arrived at the venue, we had to stop by at the registration table and drop our business cards in a bowl. I did both and just as I was about to leave, I heard her say, "Adedoyin! How are you? It's so good to see you." She went ahead to pick up the business card I had dropped after we exchanged pleasantries and said, "Wow. Brand Communications Manager. Tell me about that." I quickly rushed through what my JD was and she said we should catch up after the event since it was about to start.

That person is Francesca. Remember her from the previous story? Although I had met her before in my previous role, I don't recall us having any memorable conversation beyond "Hello" and "Hi". I was actually stunned that she knew who I was and was so warm to me.

That particular event went well. I did the posts as planned and I found the conversation the panelists had to be quite enlightening. Just as I was about to sneak out and leave after taking all the usual selfies and bantering with my colleagues, Francesca did come to find me to finish the conversation. She said we should keep in touch and that was the end of that. Or so I thought.

A few weeks later, she made that life-changing phone call that brought in my first international brief. A few weeks after that, she called again. This time, that phone call led me into the deeper ocean of purpose.

"I'm looking for someone to manage LLA's social media. I saw what you did during the event and I want you to come on board to build our vision." She went on to tell me about how LLA started, why she persisted despite the challenges and the future plans she had. It was huge. This was a chance to do something that was much bigger than Adedoyin. As I said yes to her offer, I pictured the women and young girls we were going to impact and felt a rush of joy.

Handling LLA's social media required deep research and creative skills to dig out and tell the stories of young women across Africa who were doing ground-breaking things; women who achieved much despite having only very little, women who didn't let societal and traditional limitations hold them back. There were stories that made me laugh; others left me speechless while some made me cry. "Why are some societies so cruel to women?" But I saw a common thread in these stories; a determination to make a difference and a passion to change the narrative for those coming behind.

Aside from LLA, I started to take on other side briefs. Remember I wanted to supplement the income I received from my part-time job. I received a flood of requests to manage communications for different brands. With each brief, the pay got significantly better and my account balance was at a decent level. The downside to all of this was that I soon began to stretch myself too thin. I was barely sleeping at this point. Work consumed my entire life. You could always find me typing away on my laptop or 'pressing phone' like my mother would say. Although things were looking up, I still felt empty.

The only brief that was intertwined with my inner sense of purpose was LLA. Francesca's passion, faith and vision rubbed off on me. I said yes to any request or plan she had before I even considered how tasking it would be to execute. It didn't matter because one of the things I learnt from Francesca has proved to be true over time – there is always a way. Always. Sometimes, you have to think out of the box. Other times, you have to ask for divine intervention but no matter what, you should never give up on a dream on the first sight of obstacles.

Another highlight in this period was curating the 100 Most Inspiring Women in Nigeria list. I had known about the list but for the first time, I saw the hard work and thought that went into putting it together. Every year since 2016, I have counted it a privilege to be able to join the LLA team to put this list together. It's not just about celebrating women who are doing amazing work in different fields, it's also about celebrating the fact that you do not need to be in a power suit, have a nice office and speak the best English to make an impact. Every year, I have been awed by the diversity of women across Nigeria smashing ceilings in the corporate world, public sector, social sector, rural communities and so on.

Beyond LLA, Francesca had become a strong pillar in my life and a voice that called out the gifted Adedoyin that wanted to remain hidden. She encouraged me, held my hand, affirmed me and opened doors for me. She saw what I didn't see in myself at that time and she didn't fail to let me know how great she thought I was. I didn't know it then but she was sowing seeds into my heart that eventually provided an enabling environment for me to bloom according to God's plan.

After spending years oscillating between the pursuit of money and purpose, I decided to leave the hustle behind. My plan was to dive fully into the world of entrepreneurship but I resolved to be led by God concerning briefs and projects I took on, not money. This meant that I walked away from quite a number of briefs. It also meant that impact and alignment to my values became critical. If it had no impactful end goal, if it didn't align with my values, I didn't bother. I didn't have an insane amount of money but I had peace. I had joy and I often went to bed with a smile on my face because I was using my words to change lives. I was making a difference!

LLA allowed me to immerse myself in the ocean of purpose. The icing on the cake for me was when we did the LLA 100 Women Gala. I think I cried that evening - seeing the women with their brightly lit faces and listening to their shaky voices as they expressed their shock at being celebrated for that little 'something' they started out of passion. The little set in motion the liberation of other women and young girls. The little made a way for kids in less privileged communities to go to school. The little empowered women to start businesses that would eventually lift their families out of poverty. The little did much because purpose breathed on it.

Adedoyin's Nuggets

There is a higher calling to your professional pursuit that goes beyond the money you earn, the title you have and the organization you work with. That calling is impact. That calling is purpose.

You must stand back and consider how what you do impacts the people around and beyond you. You must ask yourself, "What can I do to make a difference with the gift and skills that I have?"

Don't overthink this purpose thing. Start by identifying a need and see how you can use your gift to meet that need. Think of ways you can use your skills to serve others; to pull them up and give them hope.

Your profession is a platform – a platform to impact humanity. That is the higher calling.

The money move that really wasn't gold

"I have filled the role but will you be interested in managing the digital arm of the firm?"

For someone who was motivated by the desire to never be broke or have to depend on anyone for money, these words were music to my ears. It was a chance to make big money working on big international briefs. Finally, the striking gold moment had come. That's what I believed but that wasn't the reality that unfolded over a period of six months.

One year into my Brand Communications Manager role, I wanted to focus on bringing all the side hustles under one umbrella and I wanted to have the opportunity to explore the ever-increasing opportunities without the restriction of going to an office three times a week. By January 2016, I had transitioned fully into working remotely and six months after that, I had sent in my resignation letter. It was time to hustle! It was a move that wasn't properly thought out but I'll share that story later.

After months of winging it, getting broke and falling ill, I saw an opportunity to apply for a role as the Editor of a luxury magazine. I saw the words "luxury" and thought to myself, "The pay will definitely be good." My first role had prepared me so I knew I had the experience. I applied but I was later informed that someone else was selected for the role. However, another opportunity was presented to me to manage the digital arm of a very successful Public Relations firm.

My eyes popped as I thought about it. "This is huge!" Between you and I, I was motivated by the money and the career prospects. Even when the monthly pay wasn't as high as I was expecting, I was won over by the potential of having my professional portfolio filled with a weighty line-up of global brands.

"I can definitely do this." My mind had gone far thinking of where this role could possibly take me; the open doors, the prestige, all that good stuff. There was however one little hitch – my spirit. Deep down, I knew this wasn't for me. There was just this sense that I was going off track again. I was so blindsided by material gain that I forsook the path of purpose. But I shrugged it off. Surely, God's plan is for me to succeed and live the best life, right?

And so I started early in the New Year, ready to give my all and over-deliver. The first brief I worked on excited me – both the nature and the scale of it. I leveraged all the skills I had acquired over the years as I executed the digital portion of the PR brief. The results were outstanding too. What we were able to achieve went over and beyond the client's expectations. It was definitely a good win to have on my profile.

This brief really gingered me. I was motivated by the great start. So excited, in fact, that I consistently ignored the unease that I felt in my spirit – the one that tried to let me know that I was off track. It felt like I was Jonah, running away from the higher calling God had planned for me and this role was the big fish that swallowed me up.

I did all the things I'd normally do. But one thing was missing - I didn't ask the Holy Spirit to help me. "I've got this," I thought. I had been through the process a number of times to know that Google and speaking to a few friends would put me right on track. That's what I did when we got the green light for another brief. This time, it was for a renowned global brand. "Yes, Lord! This is it." The glory moment had finally arrived and I was about to be crowned the queen of the show.

Oh, I failed miserably. Never in my life have I looked so incompetent. Never in my life have I felt equally incompetent. Everything went downhill from here. I overestimated what I had the capacity to deliver and this was majorly because I strayed from my core. The health issues that started late 2016 resurfaced. I had severe heart palpitations. Sometimes, it felt like my heart was going to pop out of my chest. The doctors told me I had high blood pressure. They wondered why. I knew why. I overworked myself in the name of hustling.

The heart palpitations and strained body kept me awake at night. In the morning, I had to go to the office – the daily epic Mainland to Island journey. The mental stress and the health issues affected my output. I didn't do the thorough research that had become my signature approach. I gave poor advice and answers to questions. "You're meant to be the digital expert," I heard one day. That expert had left the building at this point. In fact, as I look back, I realise that I wasn't a digital marketing expert and that was something I should not have dabbled into. In my entire professional journey, this was something I could not wing because it wasn't what God had graced me to do. I also did not enjoy it!

Of course, you can imagine things were quite fragile between me and the owner of the firm. I sat on my bed one evening and cried out, "Holy Spirit, help me! Forgive me for this wrong step I have taken. Please bring me back on track."

God answered that prayer. What a merciful Father. I resigned six months later. I needed to take care of my health, especially if I wanted to remain alive. One thing that makes me laugh is that all the things

I thought I'd gain from this role, I gained and then I lost. The money was spent on hospital bills. I even incurred a debt on a YouTube ad placement that went wrong! The prestige obviously went down the drain and my reputation was only saved by the grace of God.

In the middle of all of this was when we did the LLA 100 Women Gala and after months of running away like Jonah, I stopped striving and I gave in. I was going to focus on what God wanted me to do. This was when I resolved that money would take a back seat to give way to purpose and impact. A month after that was when I got my first brief for Content Craft. You can describe Content Craft as Lily Rouge that received a fresh breath of life – one that was divinely inspired by my Father.

Adedoyin's Nuggets

"To thine own self be true."

These words kept ringing as I wrote this backstory. Who are you and what are your values? God is important to me and I put Him at the centre of everything, including my professional journey. Doing this made me understand that not every big money brief is for me. It also made me understand that certain small money or no money briefs are acts of service for the sake of the bigger purpose agenda. I encourage you to learn how to draw the line and know what's for you and what isn't, regardless of the amount of money that is on the table.

You must also be aware that there is a thin line between self-confidence and over-confidence which you must be careful not to cross in your professional journey. Somehow, your confidence must be matched with the process and growth.

The re-birth of Lily Rouge. Sort of.

"We're looking for an agency to manage content for the brand. Are you interested?"

When I resigned from the Brand Communications Manager role, I was ready to take on the world as an entrepreneur. At this point I had worked on communications briefs for an international foundation, a Nigerian food-chain and I was in the middle of finalising an opportunity to work on a brief for a global make-up brand that was coming into Nigeria. Things were definitely looking up.

Since I couldn't register the business name, Lily Rouge, I came up with a new one – Content Craft. But, I didn't register the name immediately. Aside from having a name, I also had a team member who worked on the briefs with me. In 2015, I created a platform called The Sparkle Writers Hub because of a desire to help people to master the art of writing. Dotun was the first person who signed up for my free coaching and in the middle of it, I asked her if she'd like to intern with me. When Content Craft officially launched, she transitioned to become our Content Manager/ Strategist. Of course, the pay was not much in the beginning. I actually paid her from the salary I got from my 9-5 but I painted a picture of brighter days ahead as start-ups often do.

I, therefore, found myself in another mess when, two months after I resigned, things did not pan out the way I had expected. Remember the health issues? They actually started in the second quarter of 2016. By August that year, it was clear that I needed to take a break! I had to walk away from managing the international make-up brand brief, as well as all the other things I had relied on. There I was with no client and a team member that needed to get paid!

The time off helped me to re-evaluate things. I thought about all my side hustle briefs and how I was only getting chicken change from them. If I wanted to live off this business, then there needed to be an exponential increase in income. I started to think of how I could position myself better. I was tired of being paid N50,000 to do very demanding briefs. I had to re-think my target audience and the services I wanted to offer.

That was when Women in Management Business and Public Service (WIMBIZ) came onto my radar. I had read about WIMBIZ in a book called The Smart Money Woman and I followed their Annual Conference through Twitter in 2015. I loved what I saw and I wanted to experience it live. Maybe I was influenced by LLA but I knew I wanted to work with women, especially the senior executives and business owners. I knew I could find those women in WIMBIZ but how could I gain access? By this time, I was completely broke and I wasn't sure where the next income was going to come from. After a phone call with a friend, I decided to shoot my shot.

"Put together a proposal and reach out to them with your value proposition," my friend said and that is exactly what I did. I did not have any direct contact so I decided to send a Direct Message (DM) via Instagram to Mrs. O, a former Chairperson. She didn't know me and I am not sure why she accepted my request to follow her private Instagram page but she did. I still have the message I sent to her on September 8th 2016. I shared my goals, my experience as the Editor of LLA and how I wanted to volunteer with the communications team. I ended by asking for her email address so that I could send a social media strategy/proposal to her. The truth is that I hadn't worked on it at that point. After the conversation with my friend, I decided to act right away rather than procrastinate. Besides, I expected that it would take a few days before she would read the message and reply, giving me enough time to prepare a proposal.

I was so wrong! Not only did Mrs. O reply less than one hour after I sent my message, she also asked me to send the proposal to her. You cannot imagine the speed with which I grabbed my laptop and put together the proposal which I sent to her that evening. The next day, I received a call from the WIMBIZ Secretariat and by the next week, I started a part-time volunteer engagement which required me to go to the Secretariat three times a week. Everything happened so fast that it did feel surreal.

Before this "shooting my shot" encounter, a friend had reached out to me to ask if I was interested in volunteering with the social media team for the Nigerian Economic Summit. I knew about the Summit from her posts on social media. It sounded exciting and just as I was contemplating whether or not I should say yes in light of my financial situation, she sent the words, "Flight and accommodation will be sorted." I was good to go! I said yes and began to look forward to experiencing the Summit in October.

I went off to Abuja for the Nigerian Economic Summit in the middle of working on the WIMBIZ brief and that was a whole new experience. I had a great time working with the social media team to project the proceedings from Summit. I also learnt new things about the public sector and the Nigerian government. I didn't know it then but seeds were being sown for another assignment that God had for me down the line.

When I returned to Lagos, all my energy went into ensuring that communications for the WIMBIZ Annual Conference that year was excellent. It was right up my alley and it checked the impact box but it was equally demanding, especially the days leading up to the Conference. I was, however, determined to make the most of the opportunity. The day before the Conference, however, I forgot to include my business cards among the things I packed for my stay in Eko Hotel. I was gutted when I realised I had left them at home.

I'd like to share a few things about my first set of business cards. I, obviously, didn't have money to make high quality business cards but I needed them. I had a contact that ran a bespoke printing and design company. One day, he told me he wanted to work with me to revamp their communications strategy and I should let him know my terms. I didn't need to think too much. I told him that I wanted official business cards designed and printed in exchange for a communications strategy and training for his team. That was how I ended up with these beautiful cards, printed on plastic and worth considerably more than the average business cards!

When I realised that I forgot the business cards at home and everything I tried to do to get them to my location did not work out, I said a prayer to God. "Lord, I want you to connect me with the people You want me to be connected with. Do it in such a way that they won't need my business card but they will store my details directly on their phone."

That is exactly what God did. During the Conference, I had little or no time to network with anyone. There was just so much to do. The people I really had time to interact with were other volunteers who also worked with the communications team. There was a particular lady, Miss D, that I had quite an interesting conversation with. We both had a passion for writing and I ended up sharing some writing and blogging tips with her. I also met a few people during the break time and in odd places like the toilet but nothing memorable, in my opinion. A few people saved my details directly on their phone and that was that.

One memorable thing, however, happened during the Conference. A delegate from London took the microphone and shared how she discovered the Conference through the visibility on Twitter and she decided she would travel to Nigeria, just for the Conference. What a win for the communications team! When I tell this story, I always have to add that I cannot take the glory for anything. God simply decided to bless and amplify our efforts as a team. Of course, I somewhat became a star girl, the latest addition to the communications team that made a difference. And then the doors began to open; most of our executive clients at Content Craft were referrals from the WIMBIZ network and I moved from being a volunteer to being nominated to be part of the Editorial and Communications Committee a few years later.

I'm going to share one more win from this back story.

Remember Miss D? She contacted me a few months later and told me her organisation was looking for someone to manage content for one of their brands. She sent me a Request for Proposal (RFP) and asked me to send my proposal in response to that RFP. Dotun and I worked hard on that proposal and we sent it off a few days later. We were invited for a presentation some months later. A few months after that, just when I had hit rock bottom after the role at the PR firm, I received that email – the one that informed us that Content Craft had been selected as the agency to manage content for The W Community, another women-focused initiative. I cried tears of joy and started putting plans in place to officially register the business name and open a business account. Content Craft became an official business, as a result. Things were beginning to look up and the best part of it? I was right at the centre of the purpose lane.

Adedoyin's Nuggets

As you work towards expanding your skills and capacity, think about crafting a narrative around your value. What are you bringing to the table? What makes you different from the other professional in the room? Know your value and find creative ways to communicate it.

People love and want to be around people who offer value. Remember we have talked about looking beyond the money. Value is something you must put ahead of the money conversation. Value will help you to stand the test of time and offering value will take you to places you never thought you could get to.

There's one more thing I will encourage you to add to value and that is generosity. Be generous with how you share knowledge that others will find useful. See it as your way of sowing good seeds in your professional journey. You never know how those seeds will sprout.

The Sweet and Sour Sauce

"I didn't hear anything you said; I was distracted by your red lipstick."

When I plunged into the waters of entrepreneurship, I knew I wanted to work with women or on women-focused briefs but I didn't rule out working with men. As long as it checked the right boxes, I went for a brief. Despite this, 85% of my clients were women and maybe that is the reason why I didn't have too many encounters with men who were unprofessional. A few however stood out – like the one who told me he was distracted by my lipstick during a pitch.

This pitch was interesting because I did it in collaboration with a friend. It was actually his brief but he realised he needed to have someone that was good with communications to execute that part of the brief. And that's how we started to work on this brief that included branding, public relations, product photography and commercials. This was a big brief for my friend so we prepared hard to win over the client.

On the day of the meeting, we arrived at the Lekki office early and settled comfortably in the reception as we waited to be ushered into the boardroom for the pitch. I remember how on point our pitch deck was. By this time, I was a pro at using Canva and the deck was brilliantly designed. I thought it was a work of art. Ok, enough of tooting my horn!

When the CEO finally arrived (after keeping us waiting for hours), we delved into our pitch. Since it was his, we decided that my friend would handle the presentation and I would jump in where necessary. He gave what I considered to be a fantastic presentation of our ideas and how we planned to execute. The CEO was expressionless so I couldn't tell whether he was impressed or not. He stayed silent for a while, stared at me and asked me a question that really should have been directed to my friend. I remember this because I had to ask him to jump in. The CEO didn't give a cursory glance at my friend. He continued to stare and when he finally spoke, he said my red lipstick was a source of distraction to his soul. It was at that point that I switched off mentally.

Of course, I can't remember much of what happened afterwards but he promised to give my friend feedback. Later that night, I received a WhatsApp message from a number that was not saved on my phone. I had to find out the person who sent the message because I didn't understand why a stranger would tell me that he couldn't get me out of his mind. It turned out to be the CEO.

He saved my phone number from the pitch deck. Sigh.

I called my friend and said, "I'm sorry, G. You're not going to get this brief and it is because of me." I shared the message the CEO sent and the reply I also planned to send before I blocked his number. G understood. He admitted that he felt uncomfortable on my behalf when he finished the presentation. I also felt bad on his behalf because I knew how much that brief meant to him. The three weeks and the sleepless nights spent working on it went down the drain! Just like that.

There were other unserious clients like that CEO. A top-tier secondary school in Lagos engaged us to create a strategy for their communications and social media which I was quite excited to do. In my freelance phase, I handled social media for another top-tier secondary school that was a bit on the conservative side. The school that wanted to engage

Content Craft sounded like they wanted to use social media more intentionally and creatively.

We put together our proposal which we sent off. After that, it was radio silence from their end. That radio silence is quite frustrating. "At least let me know that you are no longer interested," I thought to myself. When clients go silent, it becomes tricky to know how long and how persistently you should follow up before it becomes pestering. After several unreturned emails and phone calls, we decided to move on. It was painful because we had invested creative energy and time on that proposal.

Aside from dealing with unserious clients, I also had to deal with briefs that went sour because I didn't consider certain pieces of the puzzle when we pitched our service to some clients. One particularly stands out. It was when we launched our Personal Brand Communications Service (PBC Service). This service was actually created to help senior executives to have a strong digital footprint without going through the stress of being present on social media every day. I started to work with some senior executives, handling their personal communications needs such as writing speeches, thought leadership articles, and live posting on their social media pages during their speaking engagements. That was going well but I felt we could offer more and we launched into Personal Brand/ Image Management and to get our very first client, let's just say I over-promised which in turn meant that I under-delivered.

The major problem was that I didn't take into account third-party costs and how time consuming it would be for us. By this time, I had three full-time staff on the team and we really did have our hands full. Our PBC Service included website design, content creation and distribution, thought leadership and pitching. Looking back, what we charged in the first six months of launching this service did not make sense and we ran into trouble because of that. In fact, we made quite a few losses on those early briefs because costs we didn't anticipate came up and I didn't want to pass them on to the client after an agreement had been signed with an approved budget. I had to deal with emails from clients highlighting their dissatisfaction. I felt bad and tried to do my best to remedy the situation. Most importantly, I began to speak to other experts on the art of pricing. Remember I mentioned how I struggled with this? It affected our operations in Content Craft. I knew there was a problem when I ran into an acquaintance who had started something similar and she shared how she charged more than five times what we charged for the PBC Service and she didn't even deliver as much as we offered!

Writing this backstory, I've had to ask myself, "Adedoyin, do you have any regrets?" I can't say that I'd use the words 'regret' to describe it but there were a few briefs that I wish we hadn't dabbled into because they were not profitable, neither did we have the time for them. I took on those briefs because I saw the potential for impact. There was the one targeted at women in public service that I was in love with their vision and I took it on despite the minute budget. It was nearly impossible to execute because the Founder required much from us, especially me, and I personally didn't have the time to commit to it. The team member assigned to the brief struggled because of this and it just fell apart. There were some briefs that started well but something went wrong along the line. I could have made a better effort in ensuring those relationships didn't go sour but I didn't.

Perhaps, one particular brief that is still painful even as I write is the one that led us to incur a significant loss, despite all the hard work we put into it. The client was quite demanding and equally hard to please. That I could deal with. What I couldn't deal with was the way the CEO called for frivolous meetings frequently and changed his mind quickly! We'd make all these pitches, secure great placements, only for him to call me to tell me that he didn't think he wanted to spend that amount of money – after approving the budget. This happened over and over.

From the unserious clients to the briefs that went sour, I made sure I learnt from my mistakes. I tried to be better – to be a better entrepreneur and a better boss too. And the wins more than made up for the few sour ones. Aside from The W Community, we had a string of female-focused brands that I enjoyed working with: Women Inspiring Impact Network (WiiN), Association of Professional Women Bankers, Sebeccly Cancer Care, amongst many others. We had several corporate organizations that we were proud of the work we did for them. Perhaps, the work we did for our private clients through the PBC Service (the refined version of it), some of whom are still close contacts today, stands out most in our hall of fame of achievements and they brought me into the spotlight.

Sweet and sour, high and low, every story is a fine thread in the fabric of Content Craft. Every story is a reminder that the journey wasn't perfect but we overcame! After all, we did successfully carve a niche for ourselves through the PBC Service and our work with senior executives.

Adedoyin's Nuggets

Nobody enjoys failing. I used to be very hard on myself whenever I made mistakes. Those sour briefs were hard for me to process emotionally; I let that client down and I let myself down too. But I couldn't wallow in a pity party for too long. I had to pick myself up, look ahead and figure the way out.

Failure is heavy and missing the mark can be costly but you must have your eyes on the ball. It's okay to cry. It's okay to scream (by yourself please; don't scream at people!). After you do all of this, you must wipe your tears, find the thing that gives you joy and forge ahead.

Again, understand that the journey is not perfect. No matter how much you prepare, there are times you will fall and fail. Mark the places where you fall, take note of the bruises and punches and do what you can to rise above them. Most importantly, be determined not to be defined by them.

SECTION FOUR

SUCCESS AND THE SPOTLIGHT

You won't believe we winged this brief!

"I have a brief for you and it is a book launch."

From the early days of my professional journey, I've always been upfront about how uncomfortable I feel about selling things to people. The 'hawking magazine stunt' was what I consider to be a once in a lifetime situation. What that meant for me as an entrepreneur was that I was not keen on doing cold pitches or proposals. I wanted new clients to come to me or find me. Somehow.

God graciously granted this desire. I don't remember sending off cold proposals to any organization or individual. All the proposals we created and sent out were usually requests that resulted from referrals. Referrals. We certainly had plenty of those and I am grateful for every referral we received.

It, therefore, was not strange for Miss C to call to inform me that she had referred me to Mrs. R and she wanted me to handle the launch of a book she had just published. In a general sense, that brief was something I could handle. I had worked on the launch of a book called The Pressure Cooker. The only catch was that I was the Project Manager for that brief. Although I knew the elements of putting together a book launch and creating publicity for it, I didn't have experience with media relations. In fact, up until that point, I had avoided core media relations briefs. Our focus in Content Craft was content and social media management.

"How can I make this work?" I thought to myself.

I decided to outsource the media relations side of it to someone who could handle it. That was the only way I could take on the brief. I called someone I was confident would do an excellent job and we agreed on the media platforms to be engaged and other details.

Just as Mrs. R approved the proposal and budget for the launch, communication lines went off with the person I wanted to collaborate with. It was too late to tell Mrs. R that we could no longer do the brief and I found myself in what looked like yet another potential mess. I remember being calm as I informed the team member assigned to the brief of the new development. "We will go ahead and God will lead us."

One morning, I did what I usually don't like to do. I sent an email to the owner of one of the top-tier print newspapers and I pitched Mrs. R to be featured on the cover of the newspaper. The worst that'd have happened was that he would have ignored my email, right? Thankfully, he didn't and in less than a week, plans were in motion for the feature.

The first thing we needed to do was a photo shoot. I had good experience with that from my magazine publishing days. I couldn't be physically present during the shoot so I had to leave it in the hands of the assigned team member. I was concerned because this was an executive client but I had to trust her. "Make sure you remain calm, even when things go wrong and ensure that you constantly check that she is fine."

The shoot mostly went well and the pictures came out as we wanted them to. We also had a video shoot for the launch. I remember how I felt holding the copy of the newspaper and seeing my client on the cover. I can't really describe that feeling of satisfaction but it felt good!

While the win was one to celebrate, we were not out of the woods yet. We still needed to figure out how to get the press to attend the event. Around this time, a friend reached out to me to help her manage social media for an official event that the Vice President was scheduled to attend in her organization. It was a big deal for her and she's one of those friends that I hardly say no to.

So I went to her office and did everything she needed me to do. At the end of the event, I sat down in the hall and waited for her to finish the post-event matters she needed to sort out. I looked around and I saw a few journalists. If you're in the communications field, you always know journalists when you see them at events. And then the thought came, "Why don't you invite these journalists for the launch?"

I got off the chair immediately and went to speak to the one who was closest to me. "I'm on the Technology desk so I won't be able to cover your event but I will link you up with my colleague from the book review/ art desk," he told me. If there's one thing you should know about journalists, it is the fact that they love to operate in clusters. As I had my conversation with him, he was already signalling to the others in the room. The response was the same but at least, I had made some progress.

As promised, the man sent me his colleague's number. We had a conversation and I also asked him to connect me with his colleagues who worked with other newspapers. That's what he did and that is how I had at least five journalists confirmed to attend the launch.

God turned the mess around. The launch went well. I especially loved the #ToMyYoungerSelf campaign we ran on social media. The pre and post publicity was great too. We also created a social media page for the book and it had an engaging content calendar. Everything just worked despite the fact that I felt I was winging it.

Mrs. R engaged us after the book launch to create a video series around the book and other offshoots because of her passion for young people. That was one of the reasons why she wrote the book. I got an opportunity to travel to South Africa to handle comms for a Pan-African conference; so once again, I was absent during the video shoot. I was more confident that Dotun could handle things.

Everything had been booked for the video shoot. I didn't have to bother too much about it until I received a text from Dotun, "Ma, we're set but we cannot get through to the videographer." I saw this text almost two hours after the videographer's call time. One thing you learn quickly when you work with senior executives is that their time is precious and they do not like it being wasted. I braved international call charges and called Dotun. The videographer was acting like someone who had a personality disorder. One minute he's in Obalende; the next minute he's on the third mainland bridge. I couldn't panic because I was right in the middle of another event with hundreds of guests. "Holy Spirit, help me! Please take over." I could do nothing else but pray at this point.

The videographer eventually showed up, four hours late. I don't know how Dotun managed it but the storm was calm from that point. The videos, when we finally released them, were impactful and we went on to shoot a second batch and do some other amazing things with God's help.

"Thank You, Jesus!" I say these words every day and for every brief we handled at Content Craft, I always expressed gratitude to God for making a way. I acknowledge that I am skilled, I am capable and I have a brilliant mind. The truth, however, is that I am a woman who has been graced by God for what I do. Somehow, God always splashes the fragrance of His grace upon the works of my hands and I do not take that for granted. That is why I will always say the words, "Thank You Jesus!"

Adedoyin's Nuggets

Success can be sweet and satisfying but I urge you not to get drunk on it because it is a fickle friend. Use every win as a motivation to do more and do better. Don't leave room for complacency to creep in because you are comfortably riding through the sails of success. There's always much more to explore.

I've always used this phrase with caution; "Think outside the box." Maybe it's because I don't like being confined. I prefer to use the phrase, "Think like there's no box." No limits. No boundaries. It's really about how deep your mind can possibly imagine or as the Bible says, as far as your eyes can see. That is the thinking through which the well of creativity flows.

As you climb the ladder of success, remember to explore the fullness of your potential and your gift.

The comment that took me to South Africa

"There's an opening for you to join after all but you need to apply for your visa immediately."

When you are in the middle of a journey, it can be hard to see how the dots connect with every step you take. My walk with God has, however, shown me that nothing is ever random. When you follow the path of purpose, every step matters and they will eventually connect to get you to the expected end.

Remember the WIMBIZ shot that worked out? I only wanted an opportunity to demonstrate what I could do in a network that had my intended target audience. I didn't have any long term goal beyond that. At the time, Ms. M led the activities at the

WIMBIZ secretariat and I had to interact with her quite a bit. While she was strict, I loved her ability to ruthlessly execute – no details missed.

I wasn't particularly close to Ms. M and I was quite surprised when she called one day for us to discuss her new role. I didn't mind and so I said yes. We had a great conversation that day and she told me all about the African Philanthropy Forum (APF). I was fascinated by the fact that philanthropists across Africa were deliberately being engaged to collaboratively solve the problems we have in the continent and bring Africa into her full potential. With Ms. M on board, I knew she was about to take their vision a notch higher.

Ms. M invited me to support the overarching vision. While I couldn't commit to a full-time engagement because this was the point where I wanted to try my hands at being an entrepreneur, I told her that I'd volunteer and be there whenever she needed me. With the internal communications manager, I created an initial communications and social media strategy for the organization. A few weeks down the line, Ms. M called to ask if I had a British passport or a South African visa. There was an event that was to hold in South Africa some days later and she wanted to know if I could go.

An opportunity to travel abroad to manage communications for an event? Count me in! The problem, however, was that I did not have a British passport, neither did I have a South African visa. The more I tried to find out what it would take to apply and how fast I could get the visa, the more it dawned on me that it would be nearly impossible for me to make the trip. I had to tell Ms. M that I could manage it remotely since the event was going to be livestreamed and that is what I did. Deep within me though, I was disappointed!

Some weeks after this event, the APF had its first annual conference which I had a great time working on with the internal communications team. We all worked well together and had great conversations about our individual walk with God. There were regional events here and there in different African countries that I was happy to support remotely but I secretly prayed for an opportunity to travel with the APF team.

That's why when I saw Ms. M walk into the hall during Mrs. R's book launch, I just had to shoot my shot and give advance notice of my availability. Just in case. "I see that the APF Annual Conference is taking place in South Africa this year. Please let me know on time if you need me on board so that I can apply for my visa." This conversation happened on the first day of July in 2018. Ms. M laughed and told me that only a few people were travelling. I was partly joking when I made that statement because I was scheduled to go on holiday exactly two weeks later. With all I heard about the South African visa application process, I couldn't risk missing the holiday because my passport was stuck at the embassy. However, there was another part of me that said, "Why not?"

I, therefore, was not disappointed by Ms. M's response. In fact, I was eagerly counting down the days to my trip to Dubai – my first real holiday in years. One that really did happen by divine intervention. Little did I know that God had even more in store.

A few days after that conversation with Ms. M, she called me to tell me that it turned out that she'd need me in South Africa after all. My excitement was contained because this conversation happened Thursday evening. My trip to Dubai was now barely 10 days away. I spoke to a few friends about it. I had to weigh the risk of submitting a visa application. The company I booked the holiday with told me I needed to have an appointment and it was unlikely that I would get one before my Dubai trip.

The next day, I had a meeting with Francesca in her office and we talked about it. She was already on 'Team You Need a Holiday.' I couldn't make a decision then because I still had to wait for feedback from Ms. M. She eventually called around 5pm that Friday to inform me that all the supporting documents would be sent to me over the weekend and I should go to the visa centre on Monday. I told her about my trip which, at this point, was now 'next weekend'. She said, "Adedoyin, whatever decision you take is fine."

I was somewhere in Victoria Island when I had this conversation with Ms. M. I couldn't get an Uber or Bolt back to the mainland because it was now rush hour and so I decided to walk to the junction to look for a yellow cab. As I walked, I spoke to God, "You really need to show me what to do. Do You want me to pass on this or do You want me to go for it?"

As I got to the the junction, I looked across the road and saw a Diamond Bank building. "You can walk in and ask them for your bank statement," the inner, calm voice suggested. I didn't think twice; I just went for it. Of course, they were already closed by this time but I begged the security guard. "Please, I just need my bank statement printed to take to the embassy on Monday," I pleaded. He looked at me, went inside and came back to let me in. A few minutes later I walked out with my bank statement duly stamped.

Over the weekend, I was able to get a yellow fever card and all the other documents I needed to include with my application. I moved from one level of favour to the next. When Monday arrived, I boldly went to the visa processing centre with no appointment. "Madam, where is your appointment letter?" That was the first question I was asked. Of course I didn't have one! I was asked to stand aside to allow people who actually had appointments to go in. After a long wait and perhaps as a result of sympathy on the part of the officials there, I was allowed to go in. One hurdle crossed! A few hours later, I completed the entire process and I left. I remember praying as I got to the final submission point, "Father God, this passport will come back in time for me to travel to Dubai on Sunday."

You could call it boldness and you could also call it a gamble but I had peace. The next day, in the evening, I received an alert that my passport was ready for collection. "Haay God! Was my application rejected?" I didn't understand how I had received that response so soon!" I was a bit apprehensive as I went back to the visa processing centre the next day. With shaky hands and a pounding heart, I opened the package that had my passport. I couldn't believe my eyes when I opened it. There it was. The visa. Nicely stamped, with my name on it. If not for the likely possibility of being thrown out for inappropriate behaviour, I would have screamed and jumped around. I waited until I got outside the room and I let out measured screams. I couldn't believe it. After I return from Dubai, I would go to South Africa some days later? I didn't see that coming at all.

The journey to South Africa was great. I was refreshed from my holiday and eager to visit another new country. The intellectual engagement at APF conferences and events always excite me. One thing working on high level engagements for the APF and the NESG did for me was to give me deeper insights into the development and the public sectors, especially with regards to the key role that communications plays in the policy creation and implementation process.

This particular brief was even more interesting because we had to make the conference a trending conversation in three countries; a feat we achieved through collaboration and hard work! I visited some nice places in Johannesburg and I also had time for some shopping. All of that made up for the usual stress that comes with handling briefs of that scale but I didn't mind. To crown it all, I got to watch an NBA Africa game live. I had no idea who was playing but I screamed when everyone on my side of the stadium screamed!

This trip, everything I learnt from the conference and a divine conversation I had during the post-event debrief, remains a key highlight of my professional journey – a timely reminder that truly, impossible is nothing.

Adedoyin's Nuggets

Sometimes, I think about what would have happened if I didn't take the step to go into the banking hall that Friday evening. It made sense not to take such a risk. The data was there and past experiences of other Nigerian travellers validated the fact that it was highly probable that my passport would be stuck at that visa processing centre for weeks.

But I defied the odds. I dared to trust that inner voice that told me to go for it. And it turned out better than I could have ever imagined.

There are moments that will require you to defy the odds in your professional journey. Some refer to them as 'defining moments'. They don't come too often but when they do come and you align, they take you into a realm where you become graced to achieve the impossible.

I pray that you will be able to discern your defining moments and I pray that you will not allow fear or facts to stop you from taking the step that you need to take in that defining moment.

The woman in the red jumpsuit

I've always loved giving people compliments, even strangers. I can walk up to anyone to tell them I love their smile, fragrance, hair…whatever it is that I want to compliment them on. That is the reason why when this lady walked into the office where I had been sitting, I couldn't keep quiet. She looked breathtaking in her fiery red jumpsuit and her cornrows – all back. I had to let her know!

Our conversation kicked off from there and we got to know each other better. I had no idea what Lady D's position was in the organization where I had gone to provide support for one of LLA's events but

I knew she worked there. I'm not sure how we got to that line of conversation but I began to share with her my passion for teaching people how to leverage the power of social media for visibility and impact. I've told you how it used to bother me to discover people who did impactful work but had little or no digital footprint. Just as we launched the PBC Service at Content Craft, I also started to share articles on my website and other platforms on personal branding and how to improve your digital footprint.

I shared all of these with Lady D and she responded by asking me if I would like to facilitate some masterclasses with the Tony Elumelu Foundation (TEF) entrepreneurs on the topic! In everything I shared with her, I used TEF as an example and said, "Do you know how impactful it will be for the Foundation if only 20% of the entrepreneurs that have received support understand how to leverage the power of social media and personal branding? I think they should tell their stories more." I thought I was just having a conversation; I had no idea that I was about to be pushed further into the spotlight.

Lady D was keen on me facilitating the masterclasses. That was part of her role; to bring up ideas that would benefit the entrepreneurs. We agreed to engage properly in the New Year. It was a few days to Christmas and activities were winding down officially. That gave me enough time to conceptualize and prepare a draft proposal.

In the first official resumption week in the New Year, I sent Lady D an email and she asked me to send a letter of intent, outlining what I wanted to do and the outcomes. The goal was to have monthly webinars over a period between of four to six months to empower the entrepreneurs with the knowledge they'd need to engage effectively on social media and tell more impactful stories.

We kicked off officially in March and by the end of month one, I had received an invitation to speak to the entrepreneurs at the annual Tony Elumelu Foundation Forum (TEF Forum). Through the monthly masterclasses, I also received invitations to speak on personal branding at several conferences and seminars. In no time, I became a thought leader on personal branding and communications, a by-product of regularly sharing content around those topics on my social media pages.

Prior to the TEF Forum, I was already used to speaking to audiences of a decent size. Although I didn't like being in the spotlight much, I always found a way to get through having to stand on a stage to speak to people. As I prepared professionally, I also had to prepare mentally. In doing this, however, I underestimated just how huge the engagement really was. I remember how I stepped into the hall that Thursday evening and it felt like my heart stopped. There were over 1,000 entrepreneurs from different African countries in that hall. The hall brimmed over with people who were chatting away with one another excitedly. I found a seat and I began to do my regular breathing exercises and of course, I said my famous prayer, "Holy Spirit, help me!"

A few minutes later, I heard the MC call my name. "This is it. Abba, don't let me fall down on those steps. Please still my pounding heart." Different things were going on in my mind as the entrepreneurs applauded. I got on the stage and realised I couldn't see anyone. I stood in a position where the floodlights overshadowed everyone in the hall. I didn't move from that spot, preferring to look through the floodlights instead.

I believe I spoke for about 15 minutes on leveraging digital media for strategic brand positioning. I don't know what they saw or what they heard but the response after my session threw me off balance. I got off the stage to meet some excited faces eager to take selfies with me. They surrounded me, thanked me for the knowledge I shared, asked for my business card and there were those who wanted to have meetings with me or book private sessions.

That kind of scene was not strange to me. I had seen it over and over again as I accompanied my executive clients to their speaking engagements and events. I always wondered how they managed to keep it together and smile through the exhausting requests and attention. Now, it was my turn to do exactly the same. I smiled through all the pictures. Painstakingly. I tried to remember all the names. I tried to stay on top of how many people I could potentially have meetings with over the duration of the three-day conference.

I'll confess, I felt overwhelmed. I escaped immediately I found an open window to do so. Oh, how I dived into the stillness of the silence as I was driven back to my hotel. I should have been prepared for the attention to spill over to the other days but I wasn't. I felt like a celebrity. Everywhere I went, someone would smile, wave, hug me or try to remind me that, "We spoke on Thursday evening." With the excited look in their eyes, there was no way I could have told them that I had no recollection of such a conversation. I am not sure I am cut out for the celebrity life.

Outside of that, I did enjoy the TEF Forum and when I was not panicking internally, I enjoyed meeting the entrepreneurs and getting to know more about their businesses. We have such brilliant minds across the continent. I think about those entrepreneurs; I think about APF and the philanthropists who are working hard to harmonise efforts to create African solutions to African problems and my heart swells with hope. There's gold in Africa. We just need to ruthlessly believe and passionately hold on to a united vision until it becomes our reality.

Purpose truly is explosive. Its ripple effect can be felt miles and miles away; in places you may never physically get to.

Adedoyin's Nuggets

When I talk to professionals about becoming a thought leader in their industry, they are quick to tell me how they haven't done much yet or they aren't sure people will be interested in what they have to say.

The path to thought leadership starts by sharing what you know; sharing your experiences and what has worked for you. You then build on that by honing your skill and expertise through research, training and by learning from the leading experts in that industry. That's why I'd always encourage you to be a generous professional - one who can freely share his or her knowledge and backstories, as I am doing through this book.

You never know the shadow that you can light up just by igniting a flame of curiosity in others through the knowledge that you share. You never know the heights and depths your words can reach just because you cared to help those who are on the same journey with you.

Ending with a big bang

"By the end of August, we will officially shut down operations."

For every 9-5 role I've ever had, I've always had a good idea of how long I wanted to stay there. As that timeframe draws nearer, what I've observed is that I begin to feel this unease and sometimes discomfort.

When I officially started Content Craft, I didn't have any timeframe in mind. I, however, began to feel an unease as 2019 started. I couldn't place my finger on it but I knew it was something that I couldn't ignore. After a few conversations with some of my close friends, I realised it was because an increasing number of the impact-focused briefs that we took on ended up becoming vanity projects. I'd mentally check out when such a transition occurred and I left my team to handle things from there.

Something else was also happening to me personally. God was leading me on a path to an even higher call that I often describe as the call Abraham received in the book of Genesis. "Leave your native country, your relatives, and your father's family, and go to the land that I will show you." I was on a journey of transition but I had (and still have) no idea where it was all leading to.

It started with me unexpectedly transitioning into a new home church. One day, towards the end of 2018, I received a call and I was asked if I was interested in managing communications for a 'big church'. That request was significant to me because I had asked God the night before to give me income that will come in monthly, outside of Content

Craft. I was, therefore, curious about where this conversation would lead to.

A few weeks after that conversation, everything was signed and ready for me to begin a communications consulting role with The Fountain of Life Church, managing communications for the church and the senior pastor. Does this remind you of a former role? I was excited about it and immersed myself into creating and executing the strategy while working with a dynamic team of young people. With the benefit of hindsight, I know now that the reason why this role came my way was to deepen my foundation for the next assignment.

I had my hands full as a result of this role, along with working with Content Craft's executive clients. By this time, Dotun had now become our Lead Strategist and she was leading on most of the briefs. That gave me time to give more attention to our executive clients who preferred to engage with me personally. Sometimes, I'd be in their homes or offices for hours and sometimes all day, prepping them for a speaking engagement or listening to their plans so that we could come up with an appropriate execution strategy.

It was mostly fun and I learnt a lot just by being around them, and seeing how they interacted with their peers and staff. It also helped me to get to know them better which in turn helped me to deliver better results in the service I offered to them. For example, being around them allowed me to study them thoroughly to observe their quirks and nuances. This then allowed me to properly brief them during speaking engagements or provide better advice on how they could communicate their message more powerfully. "Make sure you smile. Your resting face sometimes makes you look like you are angry. Please be mindful of that." You can imagine that I had to master the art of giving delicate feedback to do this effectively. Thankfully, I didn't cross that line of offense and most times, they looked forward to the feedback. "Adedoyin, I need you to be brutally honest. How was it?"

In the middle of all of this, I also made plans to begin a Masters' degree in Communications at IE University in Madrid later in 2019. I won't go into the details of how it happened but just know that it was all divinely orchestrated, even to the point of winning a 50% scholarship from the Africa Communications Week Communicating Africa Challenge and 'randomly' meeting a lady who was also planning to start the program in September. After our first meeting, AR and I discovered that we had a lot of things in common and we looked forward to going on the journey to IE together.

One of the things we shared in common was our love for Communications. Like me, she was an entrepreneur who had worked on briefs that I considered to be very interesting. A few weeks after we met, she called me to discuss another interesting brief that she needed to execute. "It's a documentary. We'll need to capture the story of what the brand has achieved over the last two decades. The more I look at the plan, the more I'm convinced that I need a Creative Director for this project. Are you interested?" It sounded huge but it wasn't something that I couldn't do. In fact, as she shared the details with me, I was already excited.

I said yes and we began to work on this documentary that required us to travel across different states in Nigeria to tell a story of impact. The process was daunting. There were places that didn't have any roads for vehicles to pass through. There were others with terrible roads. And then we had those disruptions that normally happen when you have a crew working on that kind of project - car issues, things not going as scheduled, last minute surprises and all. Despite all of that, I really did enjoy working on this project. City after city, I listened to the stories of women who used as little as N20,000 to build a business that eventually allowed them to send their children to school. They weren't living in the best conditions but they had so much joy. As I write this, I see the picture of one woman in particular who lives in Ogun state and works collaboratively with her family to run her business. You could see the pride in her children's eyes as they joyfully showed us the items their mother designed. She was content with life as it was and still had dreams of a brighter tomorrow.

Yes, I shed a tear or two as we moved from one woman to the next. Even when I watched the final cuts and put together the voiceover script for the documentary, I was emotional and I was also grateful for my own journey. Our lanes and journeys in life are so different but there are points of intersection in our humanity and the desire to do the best we can with what we have been given.

As I concluded that brief, one of the most impactful projects I've had the privilege to work on, I also had to say goodbye to Content Craft. Writing this makes me smile because I remember our tagline, "Say goodbye to bad content; say hello to Content Craft." We started with a goal to create good content and we ended up with a pool of clients; corporate organisations, entrepreneurs and senior executives, who we provided communications advisory services to.

Many of my clients could not understand why I was shutting it down. "Is it because of school? Your team can manage things while you are away and you'll oversee things from there."

I know it was difficult to understand but I do appreciate every client that didn't want to let go. It was proof of the value they saw in the service we offered to them.

Content Craft was a baby I was proud to birth and manage for three years. I made many mistakes but I learnt much more. Executing briefs that cut across banking/finance, real estate, shipping, supply chain, fashion and of course women-focused initiatives, expanded my capacity and knowledge. I met a lot of great people along the way and awful ones too. I cried and I laughed. I had wins and losses as well as moments that were just a blur. The journey wasn't smooth but every time I look back, I say a huge thank you to my Father and pat myself on the shoulder. Adedoyin, you did great work!

Adedoyin's Nuggets

Shutting down something when it's thriving and growing is not an easy thing to do but it's important to be sensitive to times and seasons. There's no point holding on to something when its time has expired.

In understanding your times and seasons, you must be mindful of where you need to be and what you need to be doing. God directs my life and I stay discerning to know when my time in a place is over or when a particular phase is coming to an end.

If you get to a point in your professional journey where you begin to feel a restlessness within you, in a place where you love to be, don't dismiss it. There could be something deeper. It may be time for a change of direction or it may be time to build afresh.

SECTION FIVE

STARTING OVER – A NEW PHASE

Back to square one

"Ok. So what is your plan now?"

It's hard to move away from something that worked, or a place where you've found your sweet spot, to go into new terrain. It is, however, more difficult to leave all of that to go through a path where you are clueless about what lies ahead.

When I shut down Content Craft, I thought I'd be in Madrid a few weeks later, adapting to life as a full-time student. But that did not happen. Naturally, I wanted to go back to what I knew. Plus, I needed to make some money because I channelled all I had towards the program. My plan was to call a few clients to let them know that I was available on a consulting basis. I never had the chance to make those phone calls, however. Every time I tried to, there was this overwhelming sense of it not being what God wanted me to do. I wasn't sure what He wanted me to do but I was clear that 'rest' was part of the agenda. The problem was that moving from hustling to running a communications firm, I had no idea how to rest.

What am I going to do with my life now? Where do I start from? What is even this rest of a thing?

It felt like I was back to where I was in 2012 where I had no clue where my life was heading. The difference this time, however, was that I was confident that God was leading me. I didn't have the details but I knew He was in control. After some conversations with a few friends, I decided to embrace the 'rest thing' that had followed me everywhere for weeks. I had no idea what it looked like but I was willing to trust.

So for three months, I did nothing but have prolonged retreat times with God. It started out being weird. Many times, I was restless. My hands itched for something to do. My brain craved the complexity of a creative brief. But I was determined to stay the course and in no time, I fell in love with this rest season. There's something about pulling away from the noise of the world and spending time in deep fellowship with God. Illuminating is the word I can use to describe it. I also felt light. Yes, there were bills to pay but I was not under pressure. It was just me and God.

When I started to think of how I would explain to people that I was doing nothing, a mentor said something that was completely liberating. "Adedoyin, you are on a journey of transition. You don't have to explain your journey to anyone. They'd understand when everything eventually unfolds." That's why only a few people knew I had shut down Content Craft. Also, only a few people knew that I didn't have a solid plan. What I knew was that I was following God on this adventure and that in itself was sufficient.

Few months later, that adventure took me to the Nigerian Economic Summit Group (NESG) for an internship. You see why I named this chapter 'Back to square one'? It really did feel like I was going through a familiar sequence of events. The only difference was that things didn't look as bleak as they did in 2012. Yes, I didn't have answers (and I still don't) but I had faith in the God who had (and will always have) those answers.

At the NESG, I went in as a Writer Intern with the task to review and edit all the written content that came out from the Think Tank Operations department. There were many times I felt clueless yet again. I was involved in meetings where I had no idea what they were talking about. I edited and reviewed such complex documents that I had to use Google to understand the technical terms they contained.

Every day that I went into the NESG office, I said my famous prayer, "Holy Spirit, help me!" That is why it came as a shock to me when, three weeks after I started my internship, the head of the department said to me, "Adedoyin, I've thought about it. You can't be an intern here. From today, you are going to operate in the capacity of the Interim Team Lead." While her words were still sinking in, she brought out a document that contained my new job description. Unlike my role at VAM where I was confident that I could do a few things, this time nothing looked familiar. I don't know if it's the benefit of growth or grace but I stayed calm. I just refused to be overwhelmed.

My approach from that point was to learn from my team members. Since I loved research, I consumed as much content as I could, learning about the different sectors of the Nigerian economy, understanding the principles of Public-Private Dialogue (PPD) and mastering how to anchor policy advocacy events. Every day, I wondered how this new assignment had any correlation with what I was used to but I just had to trust God. I tell people I excelled in this role only by His grace. He helped me and showed me the things I needed to learn. When I wrote my first concept note, I was proud of the finished document. It was something that I wrote cluelessly but it turned out to be great. Don't ask me how!

While this phase did feel familiar, it was clear that it was not business as usual. Just as I was getting settled in this role with bigger tasks on my plate, COVID-19 struck – the disruption that took the entire world by surprise! It also ushered in another season of change.

I transitioned from working at the NESG to managing media and communications for a COVID-19 intervention initiative called Project Ark. Yet again, I swam in new waters but I didn't sink. From putting together the concept note for the initiative to building the brand and communications strategy from scratch, I accomplished a number of firsts through Project Ark. More importantly, I worked with an amazing team of people who ensured that we distributed over 8000 food packs and 23,000 cooked meals to vulnerable families and individuals in communities within and outside Lagos. There were of course many sleepless nights and twists and turns to navigate but the fact that we were making a difference in people's lives during the lockdown gave me the motivation to push through.

Perhaps, the biggest win for me in this period is that God used my gift to shape a narrative that led to the birth of many life changing projects. That narrative is blossoming – it has taken root and it is spreading wings into territories beyond my physical location.

Adedoyin's Nuggets

The unknown is scary. That's why most people prefer to stick with what they know, what they are used to and what has worked. COVID-19 has however proven to us that there is such a thing as 'new normal'.

You will not always be in control of the disruptions that happen in your professional journey but you must be versatile. It is tempting to cage yourself by saying, "Communications is what I do and know." But there's more to who you are than what you currently do and what you have done. The truth is you can actually be anything God wants you to be. One of the phrases I have fallen in love with in this season is, "God qualifies the called." I saw that at play while I worked with the NESG.

Don't be afraid of the unknown. Don't be scared to step into uncertain waters. Don't be afraid to shutdown what you know and start all over. Your journey is uniquely yours. I pray that you will navigate it with wisdom, sensitivity and grace.

Navigating the new: The brunch and a community

"I'm thinking of hosting a few of you to brunch to discuss all things Comms. If you are interested, do leave a comment or send me a message."

Transitions can be quite tricky to manage especially if you are someone who is deliberate about your personal brand. From 2019, I began to use LinkedIn more strategically to project my expertise in Communications. My Instagram was mainly for ministry while Twitter or Facebook became platforms for social listening.

When I started the internship at the NESG, I wasn't sure about what to post on my LinkedIn page. I wasn't working on communications briefs so there was nothing to showcase. So to speak. One day, a thought came to me. "Why don't you share the backstories of your professional journey and the lessons you learnt?" Perfect! I now had a new content strategy for my LinkedIn page and I ran with it.

I wasn't expecting to become a thought leader. I just wanted to have an active presence on that platform. Soon enough, I began to receive comments and DMs from people telling me how useful a particular post was. Some went further to share a challenge they were having and I did my best to share advice that could help them. It soon became overwhelming to deal with the volume of personal messages I received on social media.

That's when another thought came. "Why don't you bring everyone together for a brunch and answer all their questions." The more I thought about it, the more I liked the idea. I even pictured it growing into a monthly event for communications professionals. I really wasn't sure if people would be interested. So I included this side note in one of my posts - "I'm thinking of hosting a few of you to brunch to discuss all things Comms. If you are interested, do leave a comment or send me a message." I thought I was putting a brunch together but God had something much bigger in mind.

I was shocked by the number of comments and messages I received from that post. People were actually interested! "Ok, Adedoyin. Let's do this!"

I had to set the ball rolling and I started by giving it a name - The Comms Brunch. One interesting thing was that I started to receive messages from people who wanted to volunteer to help with the planning. That I didn't see coming. Sharon, Dotun and Ayobami were determined to see this brunch come to life and they mostly did the legwork. All I just had to do was to tell them what task needed to be done and they handled it.

COVID-19 struck in the middle of prepping for the brunch in March. It was now unsafe to gather in public. We had to make a decision to postpone it. I reached out to the people who paid so that I could refund their money because we couldn't specifically give a new date when it would happen, due to the uncertainty of that period. These lovely people said they didn't want a refund! They preferred to wait. These were not people I knew personally and I was in awe of how much trust they had in me.

While we were trying to figure out how things would play out, yet another thought came. I had many thoughts in this period! When she offered to volunteer, Sharon had mentioned how she saw The Comms Brunch morphing into a bigger platform for communications professionals. I listened but in my mind, I was like, "Please I only have the bandwidth for a brunch now. No need to take it 10 steps higher!" But she was so right because the next thought that came to my mind was, "Why don't you create a specialist community for communications professionals that will be for capacity building and knowledge exchange?"

By this point in my life, I had learnt how to identify divinely inspired thoughts and it was clear that there was something God wanted to birth through me. So I told my little volunteer team what I was sensing and how I wanted to launch the community on April 1st. They were all on board! We discussed the model for the community. Should it be subscription based? Should it be free? They asked me many questions that I didn't have answers to. What I knew was that this platform was going to be a resourceful and impactful one for every member.

I announced this new community on my LinkedIn page and by April 1st, we had at least 50 people who signed up from across Africa. Most of them were people I did not know and this is significant to me because they believed in me. I can't say why. And so we began The Comms Avenue.

One of our volunteers had asked me to mentor her early in the year but I didn't know how I could since I wasn't actively working on communications briefs. I saw an opportunity to do so through The Comms Avenue and I asked her if she'd like to be our Community Manager, outlining her roles and deliverables. She said yes! The volunteers for The Comms Brunch then became the internal team for The Comms Avenue.

Before we officially launched the community, I had created a three-month engagement plan. I wanted our community members to be able to interact with senior professionals and learn from their personal journey. Where was I going to find these senior professionals? LinkedIn, of course!

With determination, I started to shoot my shot at people who didn't know me. I think I sent almost 15 messages with no response. I wanted us to have the first engagement session on the Saturday after we launched the platform. You know, to begin with a bang! By the time we opened the community, I had no one confirmed. How was I going to make this work?

I stalked people on LinkedIn like a crazy person. In my 'research', I stumbled on the profile of someone who was familiar. I had read some of her contributions on the Forbes Communications Council website. She was the VP of Marketing and Communications in a firm in the US. One part of me said, "Adedoyin, perhaps you should just respect yourself." Another part said, "Why not?" Team 'why not' won and I sent her a direct message, pitching The Comms Avenue to her. My mind was blown away by the series of things that happened from there. Not only did she respond promptly, she said yes! I had secured our first speaker, two days before the proposed session. Her chat with us was outstanding. It was clear that she knew her stuff.

And then she made a request – she wanted to remain in the community! What? That was a really big win. It was also validation that we had just birthed something great. From that point, we began to engage with senior communications professionals from organizations across the world, multinationals and the top agencies in Nigeria weekly. 95% of them were people I sent a cold DM to on LinkedIn. Some moved from being guest speakers to passionately embracing the mentoring program we launched. Honestly, I am grateful to all the senior professionals who said yes to my invitation. They believed in our vision and they came with the purpose to make an impact.

I'm still in awe concerning how things have played out with The Comms Avenue. What gives me the most joy are the testimonies from our community members. We do all we do at The Comms Avenue because of them. I am filled with gratitude whenever they share how The Comms Avenue has been an important part of their professional growth. I read through the chats on our Telegram Group and I am grateful for the intellectual conversations and relationships that are being forged. We now have communications professionals from across Africa and beyond which adds to the diversity of our engagement in the community.

If you ask me where all of this is leading to, the truth is that I do not know. I am at a stage where I am walking day by day with God. Like Abraham, I am going to a land that He will show me. Eventually. For now, I am moving. I am learning. I am unlearning. I am pouring out into others. I am supporting those beside, behind and ahead of me. I am clearing the path for people to go through. You may say that I am a pioneer. You could also say that I've had a successful career so far as a communications professional. I guess that's all true. Beyond that, however, this is what I know – I am on an adventure with God and another chapter is about to unfold.

Adedoyin's Nuggets

Impact is not a buzzword. There's something about genuinely having a heart of service and a desire to make people's lives better. Every day when I wake up, I ask myself, "What can I do to help the communications professionals in our community?" That question drives what we do at The Comms Avenue. I believe it is one of the reasons we've been able to achieve so much – we are driven by our desire to create capacity building and growth opportunities for communications professionals across the world.

I urge you to look beyond yourself as you go through your professional journey. There is a bigger picture that goes beyond what you currently do.

Remember I talked about becoming a professional who pioneers the new? The new involves having a heart of selfless service; service that leads to transformation. Of a group of people. Of a generation. Of a nation. Of the world. Yes, you have the power to transform the world with your gift. Use it wisely.

FROM THE AUTHOR

From Adedoyin, with Love

"I'm done!"

Those are the words I uttered when I put the last full stop in the final story of this book. For two weeks, it felt like I was pouring out from deep wells within me.

I really did enjoy writing every backstory in this book. It gave me a better appreciation of just how far God has brought me. It will also help the people who say I inspire them to know how I started. I didn't have it all together when I began this journey in 2012 but I was able to figure things out along the way.

One thing that is undeniable in all of this, however, is that I am a woman who has been greatly helped by God. He is my entire life and that's why I am confident that this next phase will unfold just as He has planned.

I do hope some of the backstories resonated with you. I hope you also found the nuggets from each backstory useful.

I'd like to hear your backstory too. Or your comments.

If you'd like to share, please send them to me via email – letstalk@thecommsavenue.com.

Or via Social Media:

LinkedIn – Adedoyin Jaiyesimi

Instagram - @adedoyinjaiyesimi

I'm looking forward to reading your messages!

Get to know Adedoyin

You already know my name but I will reintroduce myself.

My name is Adedoyin Jaiyesimi. I describe myself as a woman in transition, at the time of writing this book, that is.

I wear many hats that fall largely under the umbrellas of Communications and Ministry.

I am currently the Chief Communications Consultant at The Comms Avenue, a role that allows me to create capacity building opportunities for communications professionals across the world. I get to interact with over 400 communications professionals from Nigeria, Ghana, South Africa, Zimbabwe, the United States, the United Kingdom and Canada in our specialist community on Telegram that continues to grow by the day.

I've been in the communications field for over eight years and I have transitioned from being an intern at YNaija to running my own brand communications firm. I love to develop and execute communications strategy for organizations, C-Suite executives and High Net-worth Individuals (HNIs).

Aside from my love for communications, I am totally in love with God. He is my beginning and my end. I currently run a community for Women in Transition where I support and hold the hands of women as they go through their transition season.

I love to write (obviously), read and I love food! I have a bias for everything that So Fresh makes, in case you want to surprise me. I am also a recovering cake, chocolate and ice-cream addict. Apparently, crossing the 30 mark does wonders to your body!

What else would you like to know about me?

If there's anything you still want to know, I'm sure you will find it on my website - adedoyinjaiyesimi.com.